HOLY FOOLERY
IN THE LIFE OF JAPAN
A HISTORICAL OVERVIEW

HIGUCHI KAZUNORI
translated by WAKU MILLER

This book originally appeared in Japanese as *Warai no Nihon bunka—Oko-no-mono wa doko e kieta no ka?* (Tokyo: Tokai Education Research Institute, 2013). International House of Japan retains the English-language translation rights under contract with Higuchi Kazunori and through the courtesy of the Tokai Education Research Institute.

First English edition published March 2015 by International House of Japan
11-16, Roppongi 5-chome, Minato-ku, Tokyo 106-0032, Japan
Tel: +81-3-3470-9271   Fax: +81-3-3470-9368
E-mail: ihj@i-house.or.jp
URL: www.i-house.or.jp

Printed in Japan
ISBN 978-4-924971-40-0

HOLY FOOLERY
IN THE LIFE OF JAPAN

A HISTORICAL OVERVIEW

The LTCB International Library Trust

The LTCB (Long-Term Credit Bank of Japan) International Library Trust, established in July 2000, is the successor to the LTCB International Library Foundation. It carries on the mission that the foundation's founders articulated as follows:

> The world is moving steadily toward a borderless economy and deepening international interdependence. Amid economic globalization, Japan is developing ever-closer ties with nations worldwide through trade, through investment, and through manufacturing and other localized business operations.
>
> Japan's global activity is drawing attention to its political, economic, and social systems and to the concepts and values that underlie those systems. But the supply of translations of Japanese books about those and other Japan-related subjects has not kept pace with demand.
>
> The shortage of foreign-language translations of Japanese books about Japanese subjects is attributable largely to the high cost of translating and publishing. To address that issue, the LTCB International Library Foundation funds the translation and the distribution of selected Japanese works about Japan's politics, economy, society, and culture.

International House of Japan, Inc., manages the publishing activities of the LTCB International Library Trust, and Sumitomo Mitsui Trust Bank, Ltd., manages the trust's financial assets.

LTCB International Library Selection No. 37

Contents

FOREWORD

Higuchi Kazunori examines in this work the subject of Japanese laughter, surveying his subject across the ages and from diverse perspectives. He traces the evolution of laughter in Japan through successive incarnations: an offering to the gods via shrine maidens, a manifestation of communal mirth, a commercial and vocational undertaking born of social stratification, and the 21st-century giggling propagated by the postindustrial entertainment industry.

The author presents a captivating account of rarely explored aspects of the spiritual and social background of laughter. Inspiring his work are insights from Japan's great folklorist, Yanagita Kunio (1875–1962), as encapsulated in Yanagita's 1946 essay "Warai no hongan" (The vow of laughter). On view in Higuchi's work and in Yanagita's is the difficulty of articulating the subject at hand. Definitive characteristics of laughter are readily apparent, though, in the contrast of tragedy and comedy.

We respond readily to tragic tales spun in other eras and in other social milieus. Readily shared in any time or place are descriptions of the tragedy of death or separation, of reversals of fortune, of loss through accidents or disaster. Less transferrable across time and geography is the experience of humor. Our encounters with ostensibly "hilarious" episodes in the literature of other times and venues leave us frequently at a loss. "What," we wonder, "is so funny?"

Lampoons of those in power and of social absurdities lose their exigency across eras and geography. That phenomenon registers powerfully in our experience with stage works performed in languages other than our own. Even a minimal grasp of the story line is sufficient to draw us into the stuff of tragedy. But the humor of another time and place can leave us feeling like we're hearing someone else's inside joke.

Japan's traditional dramatic forms of Noh and Kyogen exemplify the contrast between tragedy (Noh) and comedy (Kyogen). Presentations of Noh and Kyogen originally unfolded over several hours, with the Noh and Kyogen works alternating through the day or night. Noh works tend to be a lot longer than their Kyogen counterparts. They frequently deal with figures of history or of classic literature, such as *Ise monogatari* (*Tales of Ise*) and *Genji monogatari* (*The Tale of Genji*)

A tragic element pervades most Noh drama. Frequently, the spirit of a deceased individual will appear and recount the tragic circumstances of his or her death. The sadness, despair, and regret that commonly accompany death are fundamental to human experience.

Another contrast between Noh and Kyogen is linguistic. The lines in the former are in classic Japanese and are replete with quotations from waka poetry and from classic tales. So Noh, in its dramatic content and in its texts, is largely a matter of reliving the past.

On the other hand, the Kyogen works that have traditionally alternated with Noh works are usually brief and invariably comical. The characters that appear in Kyogen are generally anonymous.

A typical Kyogen work centers on the interchange between a minor lord and his servant, inevitably named Tarokaja. The servant uses clever stratagems to outwit his master. Kyogen's humor here arises from the upending of the status quo. The language of Kyogen, meanwhile, is colloquial, at least in reference to the 16th or 17th century or whenever the work in question was created. Unlike Noh's arcane idiom, Kyogen is readily understandable even to modern-day audiences.

The humor and the linguistic accessibility of Kyogen provide audiences with a respite from the weighty tragedy and difficult texts of Noh. And the contemporary setting is a relief from Noh's exploration of material from the distant past. But the humor of Kyogen is more substantive than a mere respite. In this book, Higuchi positions Kyogen actors in the context of Japan's tradition of oko-no-mono (holy fools).

Holy fools, as defined by Higuchi, played the role in village communities of appeasing the gods with offerings of laughter. Their goal was to forestall godly wrath and to secure heavenly blessings for their communities. And their work in fulfilling that role included transforming themselves into objects of laughter.
Let us note here the ever-present fragrance of death in the humor of Kyogen. As audiences view a sequence of Noh tragedies and Kyogen comedies, the death evoked in the Noh works amplifies the Kyogen laughter. The notion of laughter as a product of nervousness in the face of danger or death is fundamental to Higuchi's thesis.

Higuchi explores how laughter has served as a bridge between this world and "the other world" and how letting go of the sense of sane restraint is essential to that role. That underlines the redemptive power of Kyogen in upturning the dark yet orderly scheme of events portrayed in Noh dramas. Thus is laughter a social and psychological safety valve, an enabler of community vitalization.

Embedded in the pairing of Noh's tragedy and Kyogen's comedy is the crux of laughter as a dynamic in Japanese society. Implicit in laughter is a vehicle for overcoming grief.

Higuchi makes the crucial observation that laughter in Japan is but a shadow of its former self. Contemporary laughter, he observes, is rarely more than a means of consuming the moment. We search the airwaves in vain for comedies that invigorate the social discourse with substantive takedowns of the moneyed and the powerful. Comedy in Japan has also lost most of its capacity for equipping society to overcome disasters and other tragedies.

Rather, laughter in Japan today hews to the status quo, demeans society's disadvantaged, and helps expel nonconformists. That enervates communities, sapping society of its vital force. I find that to be the most powerful and frightening message in Higuchi's book.

I am certain that some nations around the world support cultures of laughter that have evolved over the centuries. And I am equally certain that members of those cultures energize their communities with guffaws of holy implications. I hope that the world's remaining cultures of laugher will receive renewed attention from researchers and that the findings will help illuminate the role of laugher in society.

Let us take heart at the publication of this English adaptation of Higuchi's trailblazing work. I pray that making Higuchi's work available in English will trigger the renewed study of laughter and a deepened understanding of laughter's role in our lives.

Saya Makito
Professor, Japanese literature
Keisen University

AUTHOR'S PREFACE TO THE ENGLISH ADAPTATION

Laughter is ubiquitous in daily life. And the business of making people laugh has become a big industry worldwide. But laughter originated as something other than personal giggles or TV-audience howls.

Primeval laughter was a communal act of appeasing the gods and of beseeching them for peace and safety for the community. The motivation was especially strong in natural disaster–prone Japan. Yet even in Japan, laughter's native-born character succumbed to the forces of modernization and urbanization. Laughter became at the individual level a diversion or consolation and at the social level a medium of commercial entertainment.

Scientific researchers have studied laughter's psychological triggers and anthropological origins. But the question of laughter's social and cultural function has received surprisingly little attention in scientific research. This book is the result of my interest in examining that question. My interest led me inevitably to Japan's tradition of *oko* (holy foolery) and *oko-no-mono* (holy fools).

Holy foolery was the antithesis of the Japanese way of the warrior, as described in such works as Nitobe Inazo's (1862–1933) *Bushido: The Soul of Japan*. Whereas the samurai spirit (*bushido*) idealized by Nitobe was stern and masculine, holy foolery was outwardly frivolous and effeminate. Underlying the latter, however, was an anything but frivolous sense of transcending the world of the mundane and reaching out to the deities. We will examine on the following pages how holy foolery fulfilled that function in the premodern era and how it surreptitiously retained something of that function throughout Japan's Westernization.

This book comprises eight chapters. The opening chapter is an exploration of the origins of laughter. Chapters 2 to 4 trace the development of Japan's traditions of laughter and holy foolery through perceptions of deities, through religious rites, and through community life. In chapters 5 and 6, we examine changes in the social positioning of holy foolery amid modernization and globalization.

We meet in chapter 7 some influential individuals who illuminate the subject of laughter from different perspectives. In the concluding chapter, we examine the role of laughter in Japan's history of natural disasters and come to terms with mirth as an evocation of the transcendent.

The first person to analyze laughter systematically from a philosophical perspective was the French philosopher Henri-Louis Bergson (1859–1941). In *Le Rire. Essai sur la signification du comique* (*Laughter: An Essay on the Meaning of the Comic*), Bergson examines laughter as a physio-mechanical phenomenon. "The attitudes, gestures and movements of the human body," he writes, "are laughable in exact proportion as that body reminds us of a mere machine."

"Our gestures," observes Bergson elsewhere in *Laughter*, "can only be imitated in their mechanical uniformity, and therefore exactly in what is alien to our living personality." And the author concludes that "this deflection of life toward the mechanical is here the real cause of laughter."

Bergson examines the mechanism of evolution, meanwhile, in *L'Évolution créatrice* (*Creative Evolution*). His ruminations in that work offer intriguing hints as to the evolutionary origins of laughter. Bergson takes issue with Charles Darwin's (1809–1882) attribution of evolution's driving dynamic to the blind, random chance of natural selection. He suggests instead that the driving force in evolution is an *élan vital* (vital impetus), which he regarded as the natural creative impulse of humankind. That vital impetus thus becomes the energy manifest in expressions of life, including laughter.

Reading Bergson's works prompted Yanagita Kunio (1875–1962), revered as the father of Japanese folkloric studies, to study laughter. Yanagita devoted himself to investigating the changes in Japanese culture that accompanied the process of modernization. That included investigating the social and cultural positioning of laughter, and Yanagita took a special interest in Japan's tradition of holy foolery. He contrasted that tradition, for example, with modern notions of mere silliness or idiocy.

Another important figure who developed a fixation with laughter was the French philosopher Georges Bataille (1897–1962). "I told myself," wrote Bataille, "that if I happened to know what laughter was, I would know everything, I would have resolved the problem of philosophies."

Yanagita, too, tackled "the problem of philosophies" through an examination of laughter. He sought the essence of Japan's modernization in the transformation of laughter and of holy foolery.

Today, the modernization of Yanagita's day has segued into an all-consuming globalization. And the attendant shift in patterns of laughter continues to provide a benchmark for monitoring the course of social change. My hope is to position that benchmark as a point of reference for a value system that will trump globalization and buttress the sustainability of civilization.

On view today across Japan are festivals and rites of laughter at shrines and other venues. Those events bespeak an age-old tradition rooted in reverence for local deities. They are occasions for making offerings of laughter to the deities or for securing divine goodwill by eliciting heavenly laughter. And most of them originally unfolded through the mediation of holy fools.

A spiritually oriented tradition of laughter thus continues to animate Japanese society, notwithstanding the profound change that it and society have undergone. That tradition is fundamental to the cultural heritage that Japanese are moving proactively as never before to share with the world. Japan is moving in the context of a pacifist foreign policy to promote peace and to enrich life for people worldwide. Let us hope that a renewed appreciation for the spirit of holy foolery will lend momentum to that ever-so-worthy undertaking.

The choice of this book for publishing in English translation through the LTCB International Library Selection is a great personal honor. And it is a gratifying fulfillment of my desire to share Japan's tradition of holy foolery with people worldwide. In that spirit, I express heartfelt gratitude to the translator, Waku Miller; to the editor, Howard Brandt; to the project coordinator at the

International House of Japan, Saji Yasuo; and to the members of the Book Selection Committee and the Policy Committee at the LTCB International Library Trust. I also thank the publisher of the original, Japanese version, the Tokai Education Research Institute.

Higuchi Kazunori

Tokyo
February 2015

AUTHOR'S PREFACE TO THE JAPANESE EDITION

Laughter had disappeared from Japan. We had just experienced the Great East Japan Earthquake. The urge to laugh died stillborn. Things that would ordinarily have elicited guffaws met with stone-faced looks.

Laughterless days stretched into weeks. Concern for the victims and for the survivors trumped all other considerations. People were hungry for news about the well-being of relatives or friends or acquaintances in the afflicted region. Simply coming to terms with the scope of the disaster would take time. The nation had entered a de facto period of extended mourning.

Japan's television networks had voluntarily suspended their ubiquitous live-audience comedy programs in deference to the tragedy. But the shows began reappearing in the third week after the quake. Survivors were still searching frantically for their family members. Tens of thousands of displaced persons had taken refuge in temporary shelters and in housing provided by friends, relatives, and generous third parties. Yet the network executives couldn't wait to resume their ordinary programming.

The commercial laughter of Japan's live-audience comedy shows is indeed the benchmark of "ordinary" on the nation's airwaves. Japanese appear to have an insatiable appetite for the banal jokes bandied about by the hosts and guests. The shows, which generate high ratings at relatively low production costs, are cash cows for the networks. And that presumably explains why the network executives were so impatient to get the programs back on the air.

Experiencing the disappearance and reappearance of Japan's low-grade comedy programming was an occasion for rethinking the role of laughter in Japanese society. Mirth has become largely a frivolous commodity for whiling away the hours and, at best, relieving stress. Multiple people might be viewing a television show in the same room, but they consume the humor individually while staring into the television screen.

Thus is communal laughter disappearing from the life of Japan. But pockets of resistance remain, as in the world of *rakugo* comedic storytelling. The *rakugo* storytellers ply their trade, to be sure, in the milieu of commercial entertainment. But they are not-so-distant kin of the holy fools of the past. And their performances retain a personal immediacy that is all too lacking in ordinary television comedy.

Witness the impressive Katsura Bunshi (1943–), a prominent *rakugo* comedian who has gained fame beyond *rakugo* as a television personality. Bunshi is thus as much as any and more than most a figure of mass media and popular culture. But he retains a strong connection with *rakugo*'s roots in live, in-person interaction. So strong are those roots that he embarked in July 2011 on a tour of quake-ravaged communities in northern Japan. Performing from the bed of a truck, he shared the soothing joy of laughter with grateful audiences.

Bunshi made an offering of laughter to the deities at the Mie Prefecture shrine of Sarutahiko-jinja in February 2012.

Sarutahiko-jinja is near the supreme Japanese shrine of Ise-jingu. Bunshi had traveled there in connection with acceding formally to the leadership of his school of *rakugo*.

"That was the first time I had ever performed with my back to the audience," recalls Bunshi. "But I needed to face the god of the shrine. And I could clearly hear the god laughing as I performed."

The great folklorist Yanagita Kunio (1875–1962) perceived definitive strains of national identity in Japan's traditions of communal laughter. Yanagita, who worked in government and diplomacy before focusing on folklore, attached special importance to Japan's tradition of holy foolery. And he lamented the disappearance of holy fools—*oko-no-mono*—from the Japanese landscape.

Japanese had traditionally regarded holy foolery as a bridge between "the other world" and this world. But looking up *oko-no-mono* in a contemporary dictionary turns up only such definitions as "idiot," "moron," and "fool." The notion of "fool" remains, but the association with a holy, sacred endeavor is gone.

On the following pages, we will retrace the origins and evolution of holy foolery in Japan. We will witness its near extinguishment through the process of modernization and globalization. We will see why Japan needs holy foolery more than ever. And we will identify contemporary traces that suggest a basis for optimism about laughter's possible resurgence.

Higuchi Kazunori

Tokyo
June 2013

CHAPTER 1

The Origins of Laughter

Why we laugh

Let us begin our exploration of laughter by examining why people laugh and, for that matter, whether laughter is unique to humans. What we discover is persuasive evidence that associates smiling and laughter with a sense of relief at the avoidance of or escape from danger and that verifies similar behavior in animal species besides *Homo sapiens*.

Aristotle (384–322 BCE) suggested around 2,300 years ago that humans are "the only animal that laughs." Charles Darwin (1809–1882), on the other hand, was disinclined to grant humans a monopoly on laughter. He detailed observations that laid the groundwork for the "false-alarm" hypothesis in evolutionary psychology.

Mogi Kenichiro (1962–), a neuroscientist, describes the false-alarm hypothesis in his book *Warau no* (The laughing brain). Mogi describes the hypothesis in reference to a tribe of prehuman anthropoids. A member of the tribe that senses an enemy

1

approaching lets out a scream to warn the other tribe members. If the enemy withdraws or if the concern proves unfounded (the false alarm), the anthropoid that issued the scream relaxes its facial muscles and produces a smile-like expression—an "all's-clear" notification to the tribe. Laughing thus arose, according to the false-alarm hypothesis, as an expression of relief and as a sign of safety.

The false-alarm hypothesis is subject to technical scientific debate that lies beyond the scope of this work. Let us simply accept for our purposes the possibility of laughter's origins in the relieved countenances of our evolutionary ancestors. Let us also accept the findings of experimental research that has verified the capacity for smiling and laughter in other animal species. Researchers at Kyoto University, for example, have verified stunning similarities between chimpanzees and humans in regard to the smiling behavior of newborns.

Newborn human infants flash smiles occasionally while they are sleeping, a trait known as neonatal smiling. Scientists long regarded neonatal smiling as a uniquely human trait. But the Kyoto University researchers have identified similar behavior in infant chimpanzees. The developmental successor to neonatal smiling, meanwhile, is social smiling. At around three months of age, human infants begin to exchange smiles with their mothers. And the researchers at Kyoto University have identified social smiling at around the same age in infant chimpanzees.

We could plausibly account for social smiling as the learned behavior of infants mimicking the loving expressions of their proud mothers. But mimicry hardly accounts for the neonatal smiling of slumbering infants. That smiling would seem to evidence inheritance rather than learning, in accordance with Darwinian notions of genetically acquired behavior.

The infants have just experienced the trauma of being ejected from the reassuring warmth of the amniotic fluid, of being forced through the birth canal, and of being thrust into the cold reality of the outside world. And their neonatal smiling is conceivably an instinctive expression of relief at having survived.

The discovery of the supernatural

Prehistoric humans occupied a natural setting that was fraught with danger unimaginable to modern-day citizens of industrialized nations. Visible dangers abounded, of course, in the form of animal predators and human rivals. The very visibility of those threats ameliorated, however, the terror that they inspired. Being able to see a threat grants us the options of fight or flight. Far more terrifying is unseen danger.

What preoccupied our prehistoric forebears more than visible threats were the eerie forces perceived behind otherwise unaccountable natural phenomena. That perception occasioned a belief in deities that transcended humans' physical and mental capabilities. Thus did people discover the supernatural. Ample evidence of that discovery remains in ritualistic artifacts.

A natural phenomenon that occurred in all climes and that prehistoric people must have found especially disconcerting was lightning. People surely cowered at the blinding flash and deafening boom. Lightning's frightful power to kill literally in a flash and to incinerate trees and scorch the earth inevitably invited associations with supernatural forces.

Subsequent scientific elucidation of lightning has hardly diminished the awe that we experience at the explosive bursts. A single thunderbolt can unleash hundreds of millions of volts of electricity and can generate heat of 30,000 degrees centigrade. Lightning strikes claim a dozen lives annually in Japan and hundreds worldwide.

The Japanese word for thunder, *kaminari*, means the rumbling (*nari*) of the gods (*kami*). Japan's great folklorist Yanagita Kunio (1875–1962) commented on the association of the natural with the supernatural in his essay "Warai no bungaku no kigen" (The origins of the literature of laughter). "People heard in the sound of thunder the laughter of the gods on high and regarded lightning as the most fearsome [manifestation] of the gods."

Yanagita Kunio (1875–1962) ✿

Japan's folklore is part of a global array of legends in which thunder figures as godly guffawing. We have seen that the Japanese word for god or gods is *kami*. The kanji for *kami* is 神, and the right-hand component of that kanji, 申, derives from China's prehistoric hieroglyphic character for lightning. We encounter lightning in connection with the powers of the supreme or near-supreme gods of several cultures; for example, Greece's Zeus, Rome's Jupiter, Scandinavia's Thor, and Hindu-India's Indra.

The Incas also associated lightning with supernatural beings. They believed that thunderbolts dispensed with humans who had the temerity to slaughter animals favored by the gods or to otherwise defy those on high. An adjunct of that belief was the Andean practice of employing individuals who survived lightning strikes as priests.

Lightning figures, too, in the *Kojiki* (*Records of Ancient Matters*), an eighth-century account of Japan's origins. The male and female gods Izanagi and Izanami spawned the Japanese archipelago. After the death of Izanami, Izanagi defies his wife's instructions and travels to the realm of the dead, Yomi-no-kuni, to see her again. What he witnesses there is the appalling sight of her putrefying body, to which are clinging eight serpentine gods of thunder.

Izanagi flees in terror, but Izanami, humiliated and furious at having been seen in such a state, dispatches the demoness Yomotsushikome to chase him down. The widower ultimately escapes, but the episode is illustrative of the role of lightning in Japanese mythology and of the strength that Japanese attributed to female deities.

Another thunder god in Japanese mythology is Takemikazuchi, who served Amaterasu-omikami (literally "the great goddess who illuminates the heavens"), the sun goddess and ancestral goddess of Japan's imperial house. He is a central figure in the pacifying of Ashihara-no-nakatsukuni, the "middle realm" that lay between Yomi-no-kuni and the realm of the gods, Takamagahara.

Let us realize here that lightning was more than just a source of terror for our ancient ancestors. It presumably occasioned the discovery of fire, which transformed life profoundly. We can scarcely imagine how people soldiered through the winter nights in unheated caves or campsites and subsisted on uncooked food. Lightning's gift of fire equipped our ancestors with comforting and even lifesaving warmth for fending off the winter cold; with the hygienic—not to mention culinary—advance of cooking; and with an effective means of fending off predators.

The perception of supernatural forces and the mastery of fire differentiated humans from other animals. And the two discoveries went hand in hand. Fire was a gift of the thunderbolts that resounded with "the laughter of the gods on high." The initial sense of panic and terror at the fiery blasts gave way to a sense of relief and then gratitude. Grimaces gave way to smiles, which escalated into laughter—a laughter imbued with heartfelt appreciation for the gift of life. Serving to remind us over subsequent centuries of that primeval sense of gratitude are the laughing voices of the holy fools.

The voices of the gods

We have every reason to believe that our prehistoric ancestors perceived their gods as an audible presence. "The laughter of the gods on high" was a daily reality. Witness the findings of renowned etymologist Shirakawa Shizuka (1910–2006), as detailed in his book *Joyo jikai* (An interpretation of standard kanji [Tokyo: Heibonsha, 2003]). Shirakawa spent more than seven decades studying kanji etymology. He gained a hands-on understanding of bone and shell oracular inscriptions and of bronzeware inscriptions by making thousands of tracings.

Shirakawa offers a fascinating elucidation of the ancient Chinese hieroglyph for "sound," 䇂 (rendered in modern kanji as 音). That hieroglyph consists of the hieroglyph for "speech," 䇂 (rendered in modern kanji as 言), and a horizontal stroke added to the box at the bottom. According to Shirakawa, the box-like hieroglyph at the bottom, 𠙵 (rendered in modern kanji as 口), depicts a vessel into which people placed written prayers, and the figure atop it is a variant of the hieroglyph for a tattooing needle, 𨐌 (rendered in modern kanji as 辛).

Speech, in Shirakawa's analysis, is thus a pledge of truthfulness. "If what I say differs from the truth, then tattoo me as a liar." Tattooing on the face or forehead was a punishment for numerous crimes in ancient China. The implicit pledge deciphered here by Shirakawa calls to mind the familiar Christian oath, "Cross my heart and hope to die, stick a needle in my eye."

Ancient Chinese believed that a sound would emanate from the prayer box if the gods accepted their pleas. Thus the addition of the horizontal stroke to the box. The kanji component 口 became

日, the middle stroke signifying the voice that emanated from within. Thus do we arrive at the composite audio (音) for "sound"— the voice of the gods, the earthly expression of divine will.

Communities required the ability to recognize and understand the voices of the gods and to reply in a manner that conveyed human gratitude. Over the centuries, different sorts of shamans, priests, and other religious figures fulfilled that role. The holy fools, meanwhile, were parallel entities. People in different eras and in different cultures attributed to those individuals a divine capacity for communicating with the gods.

Yanagita speculates on holy foolery's origins in the previously mentioned essay, "Warai no bungaku no kigen" (The origins of the literature of laughter). He detects those origins in the recognition that "the gods are far more fearsome than anything in this world and that not a moment of peace is possible upon earning their wrath." He perceives in holy foolery the joy and relief "of reveling in the laughter of the gods, of behaving in a manner intended to elicit godly laughter, and of delighting in offering up laughter unreservedly in company with the Heavenly host."

We also find intriguing insights into the divinity of sound in the writings of ethnologist and Japanese literary scholar Origuchi Shinobu (1887–1953). Origuchi, who engaged in a professional give-and-take with the older Yanagita, developed the theory of *marebito*. That term, rendered alternately with the homonymic kanji compounds for "visitor" (客人) and "rare person" (稀人), refers to a category of deities. The deities were those traditionally believed to animate the life of Japan through visits during festivals, groundbreakings for homes, and other auspicious occasions.

Villagers in old Japan credited the *marebito* for bringing such good fortune as bounteous harvests. And village dwellers commonly reported having heard the sound of *marebito* at their doors during the night. Let us note that the *marebito* were deities heard and not seen. The perceived audibility of their nocturnal visits was an important facet of sound's role as an intermediary between the people of this world and the deities of the "other world."

Japan accumulated an extensive lore of goblins, trolls, sprites, and the like. Sound was a defining part of the character and names of a lot of those beings, suggesting a *marebito* pedigree. Among the apparitions associated with sites throughout Japan are the Mat Beater, Bean Rinser, Mattock Drummer, Mountain Serenader, Foot Stepper, and Bamboo-Cutting Raccoon Dog, to name but a few of the noisy cast.

Origuchi Shinobu (1887–1953)

Attributing a corporeal identity to the mysterious and unsettling sounds tossed up by the natural environment helped people cope with those sounds. Thus did thunder, for example, become an animate presence. And attributing a comical character to some of the incarnations further mitigated the sense of menace. So the progressive animation of formerly inanimate sounds and other phenomena gave rise to a whole spectrum of gods and lesser supernatural beings.

Yanagita interpreted the lesser supernatural beings in Japanese folklore as audible incarnations of fallen gods. He read as a young man "Die Götter im Exil" ("The Gods in Exile"), by the German poet and essayist Heinrich Heine (1797–1856). In that essay, Heine argues that Europe's native deities lost their standing amid the influx of Christianity. And Heine's influence is evident in Yanagita's interpretation of Japan's goblins and company as diminished deities.

Well before the evolution of goblins and their kin in Japan, holy fools had assumed a well-established social role. People attributed to them the ability to hear the voices of the gods and to receive blessings from on high. And the laughter of the holy fools verified a two-way communication. Sound was fundamental to holy foolery.

The aural abode of the gods

So awash in noise is modern society that people have long since ceased associating sound with the voices of the gods. But the definitive role of sound in our social origins warrants careful consideration. Spiritual perceptions most assuredly arose in society

Heinrich Heine (1797–1856)
1837 engraving by Jakob Felsing
(1802–1883) of drawing by Tony
Johannot (1803–1852)

before the invention of writing and before even the emergence of language. Prehistoric artifacts, as noted, present ample evidence of that likelihood, though researchers differ in their interpretation of the evidence. And the natural abode for the perceived gods in societies devoid of written language was sound.

I made two trips to Kenya and Tanzania about 20 years ago and was amazed to learn there that long-range communication was possible with drums. On the dry savanna, drumbeats and their message carry over distances of several kilometers. We can understand why people in African societies regarded drums as religious instruments capable of linking heaven and earth.

As surprising to me as the long distances over which the communication unfolded was the complexity of the content that could be conveyed through the drumbeat encoding. Africa's drum communication predates the 19th-century invention of Morse code by centuries. It epitomizes the sophisticated growth and development of societies that is demonstrably possible even in the absence of written language.

The social anthropologist Kawada Junzo (1934–) explored this subject in connection with West Africa's Mossi people in his book *Mumoji shakai no rekishi* (The history of a society devoid of written language [Tokyo: Iwanami Shoten, 1976]). In that work, Kawada describes an illuminating event. He had just begun recording accounts of Mossi history in the court of the Mossi emperor when he learned of an upcoming recitation of the imperial lineage. The recitation would take place in the palace courtyard in the early morning of an upcoming market day. It would be by a court musician of the *benda* guild.

Kawada knew that the *benda* musicians recited the imperial lineage to the accompaniment of drums, and he resolved to record the performance. He got up early on the appointed day and set up his tape recorder to capture the event. The *benda* performer arrived on schedule and began pounding away at his drum, which Kawada recorded faithfully. What Kawada assumed to be a percussive prelude to the recitation went on, however, for a long time. So he turned off his tape recorder midway to conserve tape and stood by to resume recording when the recitation began.

After some 40 minutes of drumming, the *benda* performer picked up his things and left, and a young girl began sweeping the courtyard. The nonplussed Kawada asked the girl if the performer would be returning soon to continue the program with the promised recitation. She gave him a puzzled look and asked,

"Didn't you hear the recitation that just ended?" Only then did the realization hit Kawada that the drumming itself had been the praiseful recitation of the imperial lineage.

Drumming never evolved into a means of long-distance communication in Japan. That is possibly because sound doesn't travel far in Japan's humid climate or across its mountainous and heavily forested terrain. Japanese have a long history, however, of casting and using bronze bells. Constituting the earliest chapter in that history are the *dotaku* bronze bells of Japan's Yayoi period (300 BCE–250 CE). Those bells, which were rung with suspended internal clappers, remain a mystery as to their purpose.

The approximately 500 extant examples of *dotaku* bells range in size from 12 centimeters to 144 centimeters in height. Their

A third-century dotaku *bell*

richly decorated bodies feature motifs that suggest that the bells were used in agricultural rituals. Whatever their precise role in Yayoi society, we can well imagine that people regarded the bells as an aural link to their deities. Here was the laughter of the gods in bronze timbres.

Mysteriously, the Japanese stopped casting the *dotaku* bells in the third century CE. Not until the fifth century CE would the Japanese adopt a writing system based on imported Chinese script, so no written record remains of the bells or of the reasons that they went out of use. So thoroughly had the bells faded from history that their rediscovery created a stir in seventh- and eighth-century Japan. The earliest written record of *dotaku* bells describes people's incredulity at one unearthed in present-day Shiga Prefecture in 668. Similar surprise accompanied the unearthing of another in present-day Nara Prefecture in 713.

Another startling discovery of *dotaku* bells occurred more than 1,200 years later. That was in 1984, when archaeologists unearthed six bells, along with 358 bronze swords and 16 bronze halberds, near Izumo-taisha (Izumo Grand Shrine), in Shimane Prefecture. A further 39 *dotaku* bells emerged in 1996 at another archaeological site in the Izumo vicinity.

Ringing dozens of *dotaku* bells at once would have unleashed a carillonic symphony—a powerful appeal to the deities on high. Yet the Izumo *dotaku* bells evince a striking trend that implies that no such en masse performance ever occurred. Their casting dates span the period from around 200 BCE to around 200 CE. And over that span, the bells became progressively larger and progressively less functional in regard to generating sound. The role of sound in Japanese spirituality was changing.

CHAPTER 2

><—+<◆>—O—<◆>—+<—<

The Gods, Laughter, and the Japanese

The mystery of the Kuzu villagers

Japan's culture of laughter retains diverse traces of the ancient practice of paying respect to the gods through laughter, as well as through such offerings as *dotaku* bell ringing and dancing. Witness the following episode in the eighth-century *Nihon shoki* (*Chronicles of Japan*). That book and the roughly contemporaneous *Kojiki* (*Records of Ancient Matters*) are the oldest Japanese accounts of the nation's history. Each is a mixture of legends, starting with Japan's creation myth, and objectively verifiable history. The episode related here concerns an encounter between a mountain villager and Emperor Ojin, customarily regarded as Japan's 15th emperor. Tradition holds that Ojin reigned from 270 to 310 CE, though history offers no compelling verification of those dates or even of the emperor's existence.

Ojin was en route to his palace in Yoshino, a mountainous region in present-day Nara Prefecture. A man from a mountain village approached the emperor's procession and made an offering of *sake* and read a poem of praise. After reading the poem, the man slapped the palm of his hand to his mouth, looked up to the emperor, and laughed aloud. The man who exhibited the curious behavior was from a village called Kuzu, and the *Nihon shoki* explains that accompanying offerings of earthly bounty with laughter was an ancient Kuzu custom. And it provides the following description of the life and customs of the Kuzu villagers:

> Kuzu's people are of simple character. They eat nuts and berries that they gather in the mountains, and they regard stewed frogs as a delicacy, which they call *momi*. Their village is southeast of the capital, alongside the Yoshinogawa River and separated from the capital by mountains. The peaks are tall, the valleys deep, the paths steep. For that reason, the villagers had rarely made their way to the capital, though the distance is not great. That changed after [this encounter], however, and the villagers began traveling frequently to the capital to make offerings of the bounty of their land. Those offerings consisted of such items as chestnuts, mushrooms, and sweetfish.

Clear from the foregoing description is that the Kuzu villagers differed from the agrarian peasantry of Japan's dominant Yamato culture—the culture centered on the imperial dynasty then based in what is now Nara Prefecture. That begs the question as to the origin of their "ancient custom" of accompanying offerings with laughter. It calls into question, that is, whether the Kuzu villagers were of the same stock as the Yamato people or the descendants of an ethnically and perhaps even racially distinct people.

Members of the Yamato culture could have taken up residence in the Yoshino mountains and developed unique customs over the centuries. More intriguingly, an aboriginal group might have fled the encroaching Yamato, taking refuge in the mountains and retaining customs that predated the birth of Japanese culture.

"So this is Yoshino," wrote the great novelist Tanizaki Junichiro (1886–1965) in the 1931 novella *Yoshino kuzu* (Yoshino kudzu). "The ebb of the waters, the stance of the mountains. This is the sort of terrain where you'd expect people to seek refuge."

Note that the name of the kudzu vine is of Japanese origin. Yoshino is a famous source of kudzu starch, used in widely in Japanese cuisine, and the vine got its name from Kuzu, the village. The Japanese later rendered the written name of the vine with a kanji from the Chinese compound for the plant, so the kanji compound for the village (国栖) differs from the single kanji (葛) used for the homonymic vine. Tanizaki employed the kanji for the vine in the title of his novella, but the overlapping meanings register readily for the Japanese reader.

Yanagita Kunio (1875–1962), meanwhile, had planned to follow his classic *Tono monogatari* (*The Legends of Tono*) with a study of Japanese mountain dwellers. The former, published in 1910, was a collection of ghost tales and other folklore from its namesake town in present-day Iwate Prefecture. The latter was to have been an examination of mountain people from the perspectives of worshipping fallen deities and of taking refuge after political reversals. Although never completed, it occasioned the 1913 paper "Yamabito gaiden shiryo" (Supplementary materials about the mountain people). "I believe," wrote Yanagita in that paper, "that the mountain people are the descendants of native peoples who once prospered in this island nation."

We sense a commonality between Tanizaki's and Yanagita's notions of the mountain dwellers. And we wonder if the Kuzu

villagers mightn't have been the descendants of whoever inhabited the Japanese archipelago in the Jomon period (around 14,000–
300 BCE). Let's take a look at who the prehistoric inhabitants of
the islands might have been.

Queen Himiko and her mirrors

As we have seen, the Kuzu villagers were a simple people who
readily embraced the rule of the Yamato. The *Nihon shoki* is
replete, however, with references to "savage" peoples who did not
submit to Yamato rule. Those peoples did not worship the deities
recognized by the Yamato and were regarded by the Yamato as
barbarians.

Below is a partial listing of the terms that appear in the *Nihon
shoki* for the "barbarian" peoples and of the names of the regions
that those peoples inhabited. In parentheses are some possible
literal renderings of the terms. The etymology of the terms, however, is extremely uncertain, so we should be wary of making any
concrete inferences from the seemingly derogatory nomenclature.
Tsuchigumo (ground spider)—various regions
Kumaso (bear attack)—present-day Kagoshima Prefecture
Hayato (peregrine)—present-day Kagoshima Prefecture
Kumawashi (bear eagle)—present-day Fukuoka Prefecture
Emishi, also read "Ezo" (toad, adversary)—northeastern Honshu
and Hokkaido

As for barbarian lifestyles, the *Nihon shoki* reports that the
Emishi, for example, "slept in caves during the winter and resided
in trees during the summer" and "wore animal skins and drank
blood." The *Nihon shoki* includes references, meanwhile, to

several barbarian peoples headed by female rulers. It whets our curiosity about the peoples who lived in Japan before the rise of the Yamato. Fortunately, the Chinese left accounts of Japan that predate the *Nihon shoki* and *Kojiki*. Especially notable is the treatment of Japan in the *Sanguozhi* (History of the three kingdoms), a Chinese work of the third century CE.

The *Sanguozhi* is an exhaustive historical survey of China's Three Kingdoms period (220–280 CE). It comprises three multivolume books: the *Book of Wei*, about the Cao Wei kingdom; the *Book of Shu*, about the Shu Han kingdom; and the *Book of Wu*, about the Eastern Wu kingdom. The *Book of Wei* is where we find an account of interchange with Japan, in a section entitled "Worenchuan" (Account of the Wo people; "Wo" being a Chinese term for the Japanese archipelago).

According to the "Worenchuan" account, Wo comprised numerous chiefdoms ruled in the aggregate by a shaman queen named Himiko (dates and historicity uncertain). Her subjects, the visitors reported, were of great longevity, frequently living to 80 or 90 years of age. They went barefoot but cultivated flax and raised silkworms to make clothing and other items of woven fabric. The Wo people cultivated rice, too, but also ate fish and shellfish, which they dived into the ocean to catch and gather.

We also learn from the "Worenchuan" account of the Wo people that they tattooed their faces and bodies (a practice shared in northern Japan by the Emishi of the same era, according to the *Nihon shoki*). The Wo tattooing was reportedly to afford mystical protection when diving in the ocean, to enhance personal appearance, and to indicate social class and chiefdom association. Wo society was highly stratified, encompassing slaves as well as upper and lower classes of freepersons, and a rigid code of behavior governed relations among the classes.

Upper-class Wo men commonly had four or five wives, and even lower-class men had two or three. The wives seemed content with the polygamous arrangements. Women outnumbered men and participated as equals with men in public gatherings.

Growing populations, meanwhile, had occasioned competition for agricultural land and water rights, which had resulted in continuing strife among Wo groups. The strife had persisted under the reign of male sovereigns, and what had finally brought the strife to an end was the accession of Himiko, a female, to the throne. Warrior kings had proved impotent in regard to pacifying the realm. What ultimately brought peace to the land was the nonbelligerent, nonviolent holy foolery of a woman's benevolent magic.

Himiko, the "Worenchuan" reports, secluded herself in her palace, declined to take a husband, and practiced sorcery, which she used to bewitch her subjects. Belief in supernatural phenomena exercised a powerful sway over the Wo people. They had inherited the Chinese practice, for example, of burning animal bones and divining from the resultant cracks the appropriate timing for travel and for other activities.

The "Worenchuan" describes a delegation that Himiko dispatched to the Cao Wei kingdom in 238. Her emissaries presented the Cao Wei emperor Cao Rui (204 or 205–239) with an offering of four male slaves, six female slaves, and two lengths of fabric emblazoned with elaborate designs. The emperor accepted the offerings as tribute and acknowledged Himiko as the rightful queen of the Cao Wei vassal state of Wo.

Emperor Cao Rui bestowed on Himiko the gift of 100 bronze mirrors. We can but speculate as to whether the choice of gifts was in deference to the Wo ruler's gender. But something that we know for certain is that the mirror subsequently assumed a central place in Japanese mythology. Most notably, a bronze mirror is one-third of Japan's imperial regalia, the other two sacred treasures being a sword and a comma-shaped jewel.

The ascendance of the mirror in Japanese symbolism coincided with the cessation of the casting of the *dotaku* bronze bells. In that sense, we can regard Himiko's bronze mirrors as signifying a shift in emphasis from the aural to the visual. That shift began, as we saw in chapter 1, with a change in the size and acoustical

The decoratively engraved reverse side of a bronze mirror excavated from a late third-century tomb in Kyoto Prefecture; possibly the same kind as the mirrors received by Queen Himiko from the Cao Wei emperor

properties of *dotaku* bells. Small and resonant bells gave way to large bells of poor or nonexistent acoustical qualities. The large bells were more visual than aural in their symbolism. And with mirrors, the imagery became a purely retinal experience.

Himiko occupied the position of sun goddess in the eyes of her subjects. So mirrors, as reflectors of sunlight, were highly apropos as symbols of her rule. Yet even the opticality of their symbolism fairly resounds with the holy foolery deployed by the shaman queen.

The priestesses

We examined in chapter 1 the hypothesis that laughter origi-nated in anthropoidal evolution as an expression of relief and as a sign of safety. We also examined the evolution of *dotaku* bronze bells as a medium for spiritual messaging. And we have seen how the primary emphasis in religious and governmental symbolism shifted from the aural to the visual. Accompanying that shift was the influx of kanji on Chinese seals and other Chinese items, and the Japanese acquired a written literacy by the fifth century.

Visual imagery and then the written word thus became the chief media for expressing spiritual and political authority. Yet Japan's traditions and literature corroborate an uninterrupted aural role for holy foolery in paying respects to the nation's deities.

Yanagita Kunio posited a cast of individuals in ancient Japan who honored the gods through laughter. The literature of Japan's medieval period (1185–1600) is replete, meanwhile, with refer-ences to holy fools. Our search for strains of holy foolery in the intervening millennium leads most frequently to Japan's Shinto tradition.

Several religious scholars look to Japan's southernmost pre-fecture, Okinawa, for surviving examples of proto-Shinto. The Okinawan archipelago was formerly the independent kingdom of Ryukyu, and its religious heritage is a rich mix of Ryukyuan, Japanese, and other spiritual traditions. Occupying an impor-tant position in the spiritual life of Okinawa are the shaman-like *kaminchu*, who oversee religious festivals and other such events. Constituting the oldest subgroup of *kaminchu* are hereditary *noro* priestesses. Third-century records from the Chinese kingdom of Cao Wei describe the *noro* as women who exercised spiritual powers and, through those powers, asserted political influence. We note here a commonality with the shaman queen of the Wo people, Himiko.

Frolic and laughter are defining elements, meanwhile, of the Yaeyama Sanizu beach festival, which takes place in spring on several Okinawan islands. That festival is the modern-day continuation of an ancient female ritual. Women perform ablu-tions on the beach and pray to the gods in "the land beyond the sea" for health and safety for their families and then frolic in the surf.

Laughter also accompanies the shamanistic practices of the mostly sightless female mediums, *itako*, in the farm villages of northeastern Japan. Epitomizing those practices is the women's frantic nighttime dancing at the midsummer O-bon festival. That festival celebrates the return of the souls of the dead, and the female mediums' dancing and laughter bridge the worlds of the living and the dead.

Women have thus remained a vital channel for interaction with the spiritual world in communities throughout Japan. But their holy foolery ceased to command political power soon after the reign of Himiko. Legend holds that a male assumed the Wo throne after the death of Himiko and that, sure enough, the land descended once more into civil strife. The strife ended and peace returned when a female relative of Himiko took the throne at the age of 13. But people hate to let a good thing last, and the Wo soon allowed men to retake the reins of power, with predictably woeful results.

Never again would a woman wield supreme power in Japan. To be sure, the imperial lineage of the historic era includes 10 female reigns, and 8 of the reigns (6 women, 2 of whom reigned twice) were in the premodern era, when emperors and empresses could still wield substantive political power. Actual authority during most of those reigns appears to have resided, however, in male regents and in other male powers behind the throne. Two of the female reigns were during the Edo period (1603–1867), when the emperors and empresses had long since become mere figureheads.

Between heaven and earth

Yanagita's "gods on high" reverberated across the earth through thunder and other aural phenomena. And people perceived the deities as coming and going via such vertical media as trees, pillars, and towers. An iconic presence in Japan's creation myth, for example, is the *ame-no-ukihashi*, "floating bridge to heaven," introduced in the *Kojiki* (*Records of Ancient Matters*). The progenitors of the Japanese archipelago, Izanagi and Izanami, stood on that bridge as they churned the primordial slime into islands.

Pillars are a prominent feature of Japanese shrines, where they symbolize or—for the true believers—facilitate deities' movements between heaven and earth. A well-known example of pillars is at Suwa-taisha (Suwa Grand Shrine), in Nagano Prefecture. Every seven years, numerous people gather to fell four large Japanese fir trees on a distant mountaintop, cut off the branches, and haul the trunks manually to the shrine. They then erect the trunks at four spots on the shrine precincts. There, the sylvan pillars will symbolize (or facilitate) the coming and going of the shrine's deities for the next seven years.

One of the four pillars at Suwa-taisha (Suwa Grand Shrine)

A ubiquitous New Year's decoration in Japan, meanwhile, is the *kadomatsu* (gate pines). People fasten pine branches vertically to the outer posts or walls of the entrances to their homes. Tradition holds that the New Year's deities descend the branches to bring good fortune for the coming year. The fastidious are careful to place the bases of the branches directly on the ground to facilitate the deities' descent.

The great Zen monk Ikkyu Sojun (1394–1481) famously rued the *kadomatsu* in this poem:

> A milepost on our
>   journey to oblivion
>   are the New Year's pines
>   auspicious and then again
>   not so auspicious are they

Ikkyu possessed a transcendent understanding of "oblivion" as a realm unrestrained by notions of time or space. Yet he was also a man of this world, rich in appetites carnal and otherwise, and he was not above engaging in secular discourse on the temporal scope of biological existence.

Japan's midsummer O-bon festival (pages 86–87), epitomizes a deep-seated belief in "the other world." People light lanterns and engage in community folk dancing in the name of welcoming home the spirits of their ancestors. The assumption has been that the spirits move freely between "the other world" and this world. Most, if not all, traditional Japanese festivals are to some extent a summoning of deities. And underlying the belief in the coming and going of the deities is the assumption of mutual interests.

People counted on the deities to bestow benefits, such as bountiful harvests, fertility, or whatever. And in making offerings—including the holy foolery offering of laughter—they contributed to the fulfillment of the gods on high.

Hokkaido's Ainu people believed that their *kamuy* deities assumed earthly forms to descend into this world. They regarded bears, for example, as the earthly appearance of mountain *kamuy*. And they regarded the furs, meat, and other blessings that they secured from the bears they hunted as blessings bestowed by those deities. In return for those blessings, they set aside part of bears' bones and entrails as offerings of gratitude. They placed those offerings on altars along with offerings of *sake* and food intended to delight the deities.

The effort that went into the offerings was a sort of PR campaign. Deities who were happy with their earthly takings would spread the word among their fellow deities. And the others would thereupon bestow blessings on this world in the hope of securing similar compensation.

People in Japan's hunting societies thus regarded ample game as the result of a virtuous cycle of divine satisfaction and reimbursement. That cycle became more complex and nuanced among the farming peoples who came to dominate the Japanese countryside. But notions of mutual dependence and mutual benefit between heaven and earth endured.

Yanagita relates an interpretation of divine behavior offered by farming folk in a community where he did research. "When spring dawns, the mountain deities descend to the farming villages and become the deities of rice paddies. When autumn ends, they return to the peaks and resume their roles as mountain deities."

Thus did the Japanese interface with the ineffable evolve from a one-way dynamic to an organic synergy. Thunder became the terrifying voice of the supernatural. Bears, venomous snakes, wolves, and other life-threatening fauna were manifestations of supernatural forces. People gradually learned, however, to parry the menace of such forces and even to secure blessings in their stead through offerings to the gods on high. That spiritual jujutsu enabled the Japanese to transform menacing rumbles and growls into benevolent laughter.

The offerings

The world's diversity of spiritual traditions reminds us that people through the ages have conceptualized the ineffable in different ways. Divinities, generally personified to some extent or another, are a result of that conceptualization. And the perception of a divine presence has arisen in all manner of settings and occasions.

Japan's ubiquitous shrines, some no more than roadside altars and others that comprise multiple large structures and precincts of hundreds and even thousands of acres, stand at sites where people perceived a divine presence. Historians debate when the building of shrines of the kinds seen in Japan began, but the tradition seems to have begun sometime in or around the Nara period (710–794). Japanese possessed a well-developed cosmology, of course, long before that time, as documented by historical sources. So perceptions of a divine presence presumably predated the construction of the shrines at most of the sites.

Here again, Okinawa offers a glimpse of proto-Shinto. Scattered across the Okinawan archipelago are shrines known locally as *utaki*. At each *utaki*, a natural feature, such as a stream, a spring, a patch of forest, or an islet, is itself the shrine. Some *utaki* have

An utaki *shrine in Okinawa*

fixtures that people have erected, such as shrine buildings and stone monuments, but those are mere trappings. And some of the *utaki* have no such artificial accoutrements at all.

Any of various events could spawn the geographical perception of a divine presence and the siting of a shrine; for example, a lightning strike, an imposing tree, a distinctive boulder formation, or the judgment of an individual regarded as a seer. Whatever the origin, the resultant shrine and its presumed occupant occasioned a resident deity for the community. That being became a god of the land—a sort of lifelong patron saint for everyone who possessed ties to the vicinity through birth or otherwise.

Accompanying the transition from a hunting and gathering lifestyle to an agricultural one was an attachment to specific plots of land. Notions of resident deities went hand in hand with the sense of residency on the part of the supplicants. A landed sense of place engendered, in turn, a keen awareness of "here" and "there," of "us" and "them." Those engaged communally in the life-and-death struggle to secure sustenance from the earth developed an obsessive solidarity.

Having secured a resident deity, the people of a community jointly set about earning its goodwill. The invisible resident was, after all, an awesome neighbor—a potential menace as well as a hoped-for source of blessings. Monetary offerings have become a custom at New Year's visits to shrines since the invention of currency. But more literal offerings prevailed in Japan's farming communities of old. The offering of rice wrapped in paper, for example, was a universal agrarian plea for good weather and a bountiful harvest. And offerings of produce and products unique to the shrine vicinities became a means of reinforcing community ties with the local deities.

The tradition of supplementing offerings with laughter, which we saw with the Kuzu villagers (pages 15–18), evolved in numerous communities. Laughter became part of various rituals. Annual laughing festivals took place in several locales. And comedy became part of the rustic village productions, such as the music and dancing of *dengaku* (paddy music) rice-planting celebrations, that spawned Noh drama and Kyogen comic theater.

The local deities

The Japanese famously absorbed Western technology and other useful elements of Western culture in the 19th and 20th centuries while retaining their traditional religions. Modernization nonetheless took a heavy toll on Japan's gods of the land. Traditional beliefs waned amid the influx of Western rationality, and the community deities received a declining measure of devotion.

Christianity had long since displaced traditional deities across most of the West. Constantine the Great (272–337, reigned 306 to 337) had become the first Christian emperor of the Roman Empire, and the emperor Theodosius I (347–395, reigned 379–395) had made Christianity the empire's official religion. Thus had Christianity's single god displaced the multitude of the Roman pantheon. Christian monotheism had ultimately swept away most of Europe's other religious traditions, polytheistic and otherwise. And Europe's Christian monotheism had been just as unsparing of traditional religious practices in the Americas.

A curious duality persisted in Japanese culture until the late 20th century. Although most Japanese no longer gave the community deities much thought, a significant minority retained some measure of belief in the community deities. Few Japanese today express a literal belief in the traditional deities, but the shrines and festivals dedicated to those deities retain a prominent positioning in the life of the nation.

Most Japanese visit shrines for New Year's prayers. And people gather at shrines for all sorts of other festivals throughout the year. The festivals can be riotous affairs, and a lot of them feature floats carried or pulled by the participants. Those floats are conveyances, Japanese traditionally believed, for the deities honored at the festivals. Japan's Shinto customs also occasion quieter gatherings at shrines. For example, the autumn Shichi-go-san (Seven, five, three) festival, a rite of passage for three-year-old boys and girls, for five-year-old boys, and for seven-year-old girls, attracts numerous families.

In a similar vein, the Japanese term for groundbreaking (as for a home) is *jichinsai* (rite for quieting the earth). A Shinto priest generally presides at the ceremony, which originated as an appeal to the deities of the earth: Please allow the construction to proceed safely and for the family to live in peace in the completed home. Few Japanese would acknowledge harboring a literal belief in "deities of the earth." But fewer still would dare to dispense with the *jichinsai* rite in advance of building a home.

We could argue that the foregoing kinds of practices have become a matter of secular custom, as opposed to sacred belief. We could argue, on the other hand, that the instinctive responses of deeply ingrained custom are spiritually more profound than the verbal conceptualizing of intellectual faith. In any case, a fuzziness pervades Japanese notions of spirituality, and trying to distinguish between passive custom and proactive belief is more often than not an exercise in futility.

The laughter of the gods in legend

A central dynamic of myth is the coming and going of deities between heaven and earth. The deities of Japan's creation myth, as recounted in the *Kojiki*, divide into the deities of heaven and of earth. A struggle ensues over control, and the deities of heaven end up asserting dominance over their earthly counterparts.

The myths that have come down to us over millennia inevitably reflect the political and social stance of the myths' human conveyors. They also contain vestiges of ancient practices, including laughter. Witness the *Kojiki*'s account of how the goddess Ame-no-uzume helped save the world by eliciting laughter from her fellow deities.

Amaterasu(-omikami), the sun goddess, had angrily concealed herself in a cave after her brother, Susa-no-o, wrought havoc in her realm. Her absence had cast the world into darkness, and the other deities were desperately seeking a way to coax Amaterasu out of the cave. Ame-no-uzume overturned a tub at the mouth of the cave, climbed up onto it, and began dancing wildly. Her explicit gyrations, in the course of which she tore off her clothing and exposed her breasts and even her genitalia, elicited peals of laughter from the audience.

So great was the commotion that Amaterasu couldn't resist stepping out to see what was going on. Outside, a mirror held up by the sun goddess's fellow deities beguiled her with its reflection of her stunning appearance. Amaterasu's divine counterparts then blocked the entrance to the cave to prevent her from retreating back inside, and she subsequently agreed to rejoin them, restoring light to the world.

Japanese renderings of Ame-no-uzume have generally depicted her as a homely woman possessed of a round face and a flat nose. That portrayal has reverberated through the centuries in stage and festival masks based on perceptions of the bold female deity. And the comic character of those depictions evokes the holy foolery posited by Yanagita.

A tool for survival

The cultural anthropologist Ishida Eiichiro (1903–1968) identified parallels with the foregoing tale in the mythologies of other nations in the Pacific basin. Here is an example that he cited—a story passed down among the Eel River Athapaskan Native Americans of northern California.

> People were without fire in the beginning. What led to the discovery of fire was the birth of a remarkable child. The child cried all day and all night. Nothing could pacify the child. One day, people noticed that the child was sobbing, "The fire is scary." This child saw fire where it was visible to no one else. The fire was inside Spider. That is what made Spider's body bulge.
>
> Coyote told the people how to secure the fire. Following Coyote's instructions, the people gathered lots of birds and other animals and set off for Spider's place. Spider took the fire out of her body at night and put it back in during the day. The people and animals mimicked Spider with comic antics. If they could make her laugh, the fire would pop out of her mouth. But nothing they tried could get Spider to laugh.
>
> Finally, Skunk came dancing along with her tail raised straight up. That made everyone laugh. Even Spider laughed. And sure enough, the fire popped out of her mouth.

Securing fire from the mouth of Spider parallels the luring of the sun goddess out from the mouth of the cave. Once again, laughter saves the day. Skunk's dancing and raised tail invest this story, meanwhile, with the same eroticism that Ame-no-uzume provided with her striptease.

The notions of restoring sunlight and of securing the light and warmth of fire resonate with the midwinter festivals seen worldwide. Peoples practiced different rites during the fading light of winter to restore the vitality of the sun. Christmas is a good example. The familiar Christmas tree is an inheritance from northern European midwinter rites that predate the arrival of Christianity.

Sir James George Frazer (1854–1941), a pioneering Scottish anthropologist, examines commonalities among spiritual practices around the world in *The Golden Bough* (1890; pages 61–63, 157–161). His examination details several similar practices undertaken in the name of restoring solar or social vigor. Fraser cites examples of even replacing monarchs as part of the midwinter rites.

Laughter, too, was an important part of winter rites and of other seasonal rites. "Eliciting laughter at the midwinter rites was necessary," wrote the mythologist Matsumoto Nobuhiro (1897–1981) in *Nihon shinwa no kenkyu* (A study of Japanese

Sir James George Frazer (1854–1941)

mythology, published in 1931), "because it allowed for securing ample food." Matsumoto went on to discuss how that principle was the operative element in a familiar Japanese saying. "When the niggardly gods laugh, they spew out the blessings in their care. We need to recognize in that insight from the distant past the profound origins of the simple saying, 'To the households of those who smile do blessings accrue.'"

As we examine laughter, we begin to understand it as a direct, linear linkage between heaven and earth, day and night, light and dark, life and death, death and rebirth. We begin to understand mythology, meanwhile, as a similarly direct and linear linkage between the past and the future and to understand the role of mythology in reconstructing the present. Our deepening understanding equips us to perceive laughter in its temporal, spatial, and spiritual contexts and to come to terms with its role as a dynamic of mythology.

Ethnology is inherently an investigation of the interrelationships of time and space, of history and land. We can regard the study of mythology, meanwhile, as the ethnology of the gods. Our examination of laughter as a dynamic of mythology then becomes an ethnological investigation of the laughter of the gods. Yanagita regarded the divine rite of laughter as an ongoing phenomenon, as he describes in this passage from the essay "Warai no hongan" (The vow of laughter, published 1946).

> [The laughter under consideration here] originates from something far more serious than casual jesting. In people's lives, laughter has served continuously as a weapon since a time when laughing and being laughed at were of a gravity nearly equivalent to that of killing and being killed. Thus have we maintained [laughter] as a requisite of ethnic preservation.

Yanagita's "something far more serious than casual jesting" is of the realm of mythology, of the realm of the sacred. In the following chapters, let us borrow from Yanagita and his circle in probing the ethnology of the laughter of the gods and Japan's emergent culture of laughter.

CHAPTER 3

➤─┼─◆❯─○─❮◆─┼─◄

Divine Mysteries

Rites of laughter

The present-day kanji for laughter, 笑, evolved from an ideographic representation of a shrine maiden extending her arms upward while dancing. "Appeals to the gods," wrote the great elucidator of kanji Shirakawa Shizuka (1910–2006) in *Joyo jikai* (An interpretation of standard kanji), "took the form of laughing and smiling while dancing." We recall how Ame-no-uzume danced and elicited laughter from her fellow deities to lure the sun goddess, Amaterasu, out of a cave (pages 32–33).

Laughter has resounded through the ages in Japanese ceremonies—sacred, semisacred, and secular. *Rakugo* comedic storytellers, for example, hold ceremonies for making offerings of laughter to the gods. And the ceremonial laughter invariably is a powerful affair—robust outbursts energized to reach the heavens.

The religious philosopher and Shinto scholar Kamata Toji (1951–) writes of a ceremonial laughter among Japanese farmers and fishermen in *Shinto toha nanika* (What is Shinto?): "We find the custom in several regions [of Japan]. On partaking of the first harvest or catch of the season, [the farmers or fishermen] face east and release unrestrained laughter."

Eastward. Toward the origin of the life-giving sun. And the sun goddess was none other than Amaterasu, coaxed out of her cave—thus restoring the world to light—by the laughter stirred by Ame-no-uzume. Eastwardly, then, have grateful farmers and fishermen directed their grateful laughter.

Yanagita Kunio (1875–1962) documented several examples of Japan's surviving rites of laughter. One example is the rite of the first laugh of the New Year. Exemplifying that rite is a distinctive practice in the village of Hamajima in Mie Prefecture's Ise-shima district. People there gather at New Year's beside a two-meter-tall statue of the god Ebisu, face the sea to the south, and let out three hearty laughs in unison.

The rite is an appeal to Ebisu for good fortune in the year ahead. It is a popular tourist attraction, and visitors from afar join in the fun along with local fishermen and merchants. Groups assemble one after another around the Ebisu figure to take their turn in the noisy New Year's mirth.

Ebisu is the god of fishermen and merchants and usually appears, as he does in the Hamajima statue, with a sea bream in hand. He is one of Japan's seven lucky gods, the others being the rotund Hotei (abundance and health); the elderly Jurojin (longevity); the curiously long-headed Fukurokuju (happiness, wealth, and longevity); the fierce Bishamonten (warrior); the lovely Benzaiten, who is the sole female deity among the seven (knowledge, art, and beauty); and the broad-faced Daikokuten (wealth and commerce). Local legend holds that the rite of New Year's laughter began when the nearly drowned Ebisu washed up on the beach and was found and nursed back to health by Hamajima fishermen.

Hamajima's Ebisu, by the way, spends most of the year without a nose. Removing the nose is a Japanese pun on "seizing the initiative." For fishermen, that alludes to securing an abundant haul of fish. The locals affix a new nose to the statue each year, and fishermen remove it in the darkness of night. Thus do the participants in the New Year's laughter rite call out to "noseless Ebisu."

Interestingly, Ebisu is the only one of the seven lucky gods who originated in Japan. The others are adaptations of Indian and Chinese deities. Ebisu's origin, however, is subject to debate. One account identifies him with Hiruko, the disfigured first-born child of Izanagi and Izanami (page 5). Some research suggests, though, that Ebisu arose among Japanese fishermen as a sort of patron saint and that the Hiruko association was a later synthesis by the merchant class.

We also note with interest the proximity of Hamajima and its laughter rite to the holiest of Japan's shrines, Ise-jingu. Enshrined there are Amaterasu and the goddess of agriculture and industry, Toyouke. So laughter, which coaxed Amaterasu out of the cave, continues to echo in her presence.

Laughter rites by day and by night

We encounter in farming communities throughout Japan a deep-rooted belief in laughter's value in promoting agricultural productivity. And a lot of those communities express that belief in rites of laughter. An example is a rite that takes place annually at Hiraoka-jinja, an ancient shrine in what is now the Osaka Prefecture city of Higashi-osaka. Hiraoka-jinja was an important spiritual center of Yamato culture (ca. 250–710) before the establishment of the capital in Nara. And the Nara-period (710–794) builders of Nara's great shrine of Kasuga-taisha borrowed Hiraoka-jinja's deities for enshrinement there. People sometimes, therefore, refer to the latter as "Moto-kasuga" (proto-Kasuga).

Hiraoka-jinja's annual rite of laughter occurs at the winter solstice. That is when the priests replace the decorative *shimenawa* straw rope stretched across the shrine entrance with a new one. The *shimenawa* symbolically bars anything impure from entering the site of Shinto rites. Once the new *shimenawa* is in place, the

Laughing under laughter (笑) placards and the newly stretched shimenawa *straw rope (upper right) at Hiraoka-jinja's annual rite of mirth*
Photo courtesy of Tetsuya Yamamoto Office

shrine personnel and visitors assemble below the rope and, led by the chief priest, let loose with three loud laughs.

The winter solstice—the shortest day and longest night of the year—is a natural time for rites of hope. We note that Christians, for example, celebrate the birth of their savior with the Christmas festivities held at this time of year. As autumn turned to winter, the ever-lengthening nights threatened to envelop the world in eternal darkness, and people prayed for the light to lengthen anew and to restore the world to bright warmth. That symbolism is readily evident in the episode of Amaterasu concealing herself and her radiance in a cave and of the other deities luring her back out to restore the world to light.

Enshrined at Hiraoka-jinja are Amanokoyane and his consort. Amanokoyane is one of the gods who held up the mirror that beguiled Amaterasu when she emerged from the cave. His enshrinement is a direct link between Hiraoka-jinja and the episode of the cave, and the annual rite of laughter is a living evocation of that link.

We also find an annual rite of laughter at Omata-hachimangu shrine in the Yamaguchi Prefecture city of Hofu. The rite dates, according to the shrine records, from 1199. It originally took place the first day of December on the lunar calendar, though it has shifted in the modern era to the first Sunday of December on the Gregorian calendar.

Hofu lies on a fertile plain known for rice cultivation, and the rite of laughter at Omata-hachimangu is of agricultural origins. The farmers and their families would gather at the shrine to give thanks to the agricultural deity Otoshi-gami for the year's harvest and to pray for a bountiful harvest in the coming year. They

conducted the rite of laughter as members of a religious association formed for that purpose: "The Laughers," as it were. That
association endures and carries on the mirthful tradition.

The laughter rite begins with a shrine priest handing branches of *sakaki* (*Cleyera japonica*) to two kneeling members of the
association. Grasping the branches, the two let out three hearty
laughs: the first in gratitude for the year's harvest, the second in
request of a good harvest in the coming year, and the third in the
hope of forgetting sadness and suffering. An elder who finds the
laughter unsatisfactory in volume or in spirit will demand that the
two repeat the three laughs. That can continue several times until
the elders are fully satisfied.

Hiraoka-jinja's and Omata-hachimangu's rites of laughter take
place in the daylight hours. That is in keeping with the participants' attention to the deities of sunlight in their agricultural
supplication. In contrast, a nighttime rite of laughter takes place
annually at the great shrine of Atsuta-jingu, in Nagoya.

Atsuta-jingu's laughter rite carries the revealing name Eyodo-
shinji: "the rite of unrestrained laughter." It celebrates the return
of the sword Kusanagi-no-Tsurugi to the shrine in 686. That
sword, the mirror Yata-no-Kagami, and the comma-shaped jewel
Yasakani-no-Magatama constitute Japan's imperial regalia.

We cannot be objectively certain of the location or even the
existence of any of the three regalia. The administrators of Atsuta-
jingu claim to be in possession of the sword, but they never put it
on public display. Tradition holds that the oblong jewel resides in
the Imperial Palace, in Tokyo, and the mirror at Ise-jingu shrine,
but the ostensible conservators never make their treasures available for public viewing and confirmation.

Complicating things further are divergent versions of the sword's history. One that disputes the Atsuta-jingu conservatorship appears in *Heike monogatari* (*The Tale of the Heike*), a 14th-century account of the 12th-century war between the Taira and Minamoto clans. In that work, the sword is lost at sea during the decisive naval battle of Dan-no-ura. But let us put aside our doubts for the sake of examining Atsuta-jingu's rite of laughter.

In Japanese mythology, Amaterasu's brother Susa-no-o discovers Kusanagi-no-Tsurugi inside the eight-headed, eight-tailed dragon Yamata no Orochi, which he has slain. The sword emerges from one of the tails of the dragon, which Susa-no-o has severed in dispatching the monster. And the dragon slayer presents the prize to his luminous sister as a gift.

The original name of the sword was Ama-no-Murakumo-no-Tsurugi (sword of a heavenly cloud cluster). Kusanagi-no-Tsurugi means "grass-cutting sword" and is a name that the blade acquired in a later episode in Japanese mythology. A warrior entrusted with the sword found himself surrounded by flames in a fiery ambush in a grassy meadow, and he saved himself by using the weapon to cut away the grass that had been set ablaze.

Tradition holds that Atsuta-jingu was built in the second century of the common era to house Kusanagi-no-Tsurugi. The sword, according to traditional histories, was moved to the Imperial Palace during the reign of Emperor Tenji (626–672, reigned 661–671) but returned to Atsuta-jingu during the reign of Emperor Temmu (631–686, reigned 672–686). Today's Eyodo-shinji rite of laughter is a continuation of a celebration that originated in people's delight at the sword's return.

The rite gets under way in the depths of night with the extinguishing of all the lights in the shrine precincts. The shrine priests each carry concealed in a sleeve a face of the shrine deity—a face upon which tradition holds that no one must gaze. They each strike their mask gently with a fan and let out a round of robust laughter.

Among those who have offered informed commentary about Atsuta-jingu's rite of laughter is the cultural anthropologist Yamaguchi Masao (1931–2013). Yamaguchi concludes in *Warai to itsudatsu* (Laughter and deviation) that such rites are vestiges of humans' earliest response to the fear of the unknown and to darkness. Laughter, he argues, was a means of overcoming trepidation. And people formalized that response in rituals.

Offerings of laughter to mountain deities

We turn now from the laughter rites of Japan's fishermen, merchants, and farmers to analogous rites practiced by the nation's mountain people. Let us begin with a laughter festival held annually at Niu-jinja shrine in the Wakayama Prefecture town of Hidakagawa-machi. That festival takes place on the second Sunday of October. It is famous in Japan for its gaudily costumed and white-faced "laughing geezer," who wanders through the crowd while ringing a bell and elicits laughter with comical gestures. And it illuminates the decisive influence of mountain deities in shaping the role of laughter in Japanese culture.

Hidakagawa-machi is near Yoshino, the mountainous home of the laughing Kuzu villagers that we encountered in chapter 2. Its Niu-jinja enshrines Niutsuhime, a female deity traditionally

revered by cinnabar miners. The name of the shrine refers to cinnabar ore, and western Japan has numerous shrines of the same
name, though the reading of the kanji is sometimes Tanjo, sometimes Tansei, instead of Niu.

We find Niu, Tanjo, and Tansei shrines in the Honshu prefectures of Nara, Kyoto, Osaka, Hyogo, Mie, Okayama, Hiroshima,
and Yamaguchi, as well as Wakayama; in the Shikoku prefectures
of Kochi, Tokushima, Kagawa, and Ehime; and in the Kyushu
prefectures of Fukuoka, Saga, Kumamoto, Oita, and Miyazaki.
Most if not all of those shrines stand at sites known for cinnabar
mining.

The technology for extracting metallic mercury from cinnabar ore was largely the intellectual property of mountain dwellers. Devout climbers who traversed the tortuous topography of
Japan's pilgrimage routes were instrumental in propagating that
technology. And the Niu (and Tanjo and Tansei) shrines that dot
the terrain of western Japan evinced more of the mountain faith
than an agricultural spirituality.

Niu-jinja's laughter festival

Here is how the laughter festival came to be at Hidakagawa-machi's Niu-jinja. In Shinto tradition, Japan's multitudinous deities gather annually at the great shrine of Izumo-taisha, in what is now Shimane Prefecture. That event takes place in the 10th month of the lunar calendar. The deities take leave of their shrines throughout the nation to attend. So people have traditionally referred to the 10th month of the lunar calendar as "the month of no gods." And that name has carried over to October, on the Gregorian calendar, notwithstanding the chronological offset.

The story begins in ancient times. Niutsuhime, the patron deity of the Niu-jinja community, had yet to become a full-fledged member of the Shinto pantheon. She was due to attend the annual gathering of the deities at Izumo-taisha for the first time, but she overslept on the morning of her scheduled departure for the great event. Despondent at being tardy for the gathering, Niutsuhime slipped into a funk and despaired of taking her place in the pantheon.

Niutsuhime's accession to the Shinto pantheon was important, of course, to the villagers who worshipped her at Niu-jinja and relied on her for blessings. They gathered offerings and placed them before the shrine to comfort and encourage their patron deity. As they put the offerings in place, the villagers shouted out, "Smile, Niutsuhime. Smile!"

The villagers' stratagem worked perfectly. Niutsuhime regained her spirits and set off for Izumo-taisha, where she participated in the gathering as a full-fledged member of the pantheon. She had discovered the value of smiles and laughter, meanwhile, and vibrant mirth subsequently became part and parcel of Niutsuhime worship.

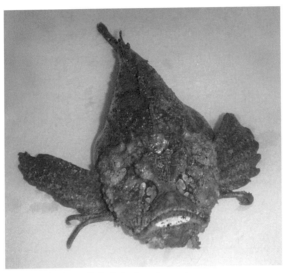

*The lovely lumpfish (*Inimicus japonicas; *Japanese:* okoze)

A mythical exchange between the mountain goddess and the sea god is the background for another mountain festival of mirth: the *okoze* (lumpfish) laughter festival. Happening upon each other, the deities launch into a bragging competition about who commands the larger contingent of vassals. They introduce their vassals in turn and are tied at 12 after the mountain deity has introduced the last member of her entourage. The sea god is certain that his entourage comprises 13 members and is flustered that only 12 seem to be on hand. Finally, his 13th and final vassal—the comically homely *lumpfish*—comes waddling along. The sea god has won the bragging rights to the largest contingent.

In another version, the deities present rival claims to the larger realm. The mountain goddess claims 80,000 subjects, employing a play on words between "mountain" (*yama*) and "eight ten thousands" (*ya-man*). Not to be outdone, the sea deity wields a word play on "lumpfish" (*okoze*) and 100 million (*oku*).

In any case, losing the brag fest left a bad taste in the mouth of the mountain goddess, and she harbored lasting ill will toward the lumpfish. Her subjects were dependent on her goodwill for safety in the mountains and for good harvests. And they assuaged her feeling by blowing off the unpleasant memory with laughter. They invite her to witness the comical ugliness of the lumpfish and to extinguish her ill will with mirth.

The foregoing tale is one account of the origin of the lumpfish laughter festivals that continue today in Mie and Wakayama prefectures. A well-known example of those annual festivals is the one held in the Mie Prefecture city of Owase. It takes place on February 7 at the Kagarido shrine. No historical evidence remains as to the reason for the February timing of the festival. But the timing places the festival just before the dawn of spring, and that is consistent with the notion of appealing to the mountain deity for a good harvest.

Kagarido is a four-legged wooden altar that enshrines the deity Oyamatsumi. That deity appears in the eighth-century histories of Japan, the *Kojiki* (*Records of Ancient Matters*) and the *Nihon shoki* (*Chronicles of Japan*), as a god of the earth, but neither work attributes any particular exploits to Oyamatsumi. The name literally means "god of the great mountains," and Japanese have revered Oyamatsumi over the centuries as a mountain deity.

Curiously, the *Kojiki* and the *Nihon shoki* describe Oyamatsumi for the most part in masculine terms (some of the references are ambiguous). That differs from the usually female rendering of mountain deities in Japanese mythology. And it is inconsistent with the gender of the mountain deity in the brag fest cited above. Japanese have a famously charitable tolerance for logical loose ends, however, and sharing that tolerance will lubricate our exploration of Japan's tales and traditions.

Gender figures graphically in Kagarido's *okoze* laughter festival. The event gets under way with the crafting of a 50-centimeter-by-20-centimeter phallic symbol, known as "the tool," from Japanese cedar (*Cryptomeria japonica*). In addition, the festival participants craft nine wooden replicas of more-prosaic tools used in the mountains, such as an ax, a hoe, a scythe, and the like, and prepare nine trays of food, each laden with nine offerings of vegetable and fish dishes and *sake*. They array the wooden items

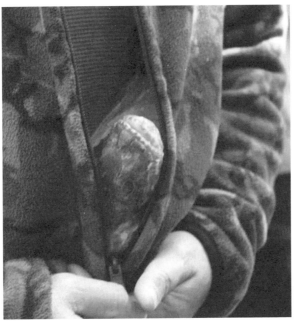

A lumpfish in a jacket, exposed to trigger laughter at the Kagarido festival of laughter

Laughers doing their thing before the Kagarido altar

and the food and drink offerings before the Kagarido and open the doors on the altar.

The two leaders of the ceremony then produce lumpfish that they have been holding inside their jackets, exposing the homely faces of the fish. That is a signal for the villagers gathered behind them to let out a round of loud laughter.

The lumpfish rites and Yanagita Kunio

Yanagita Kunio possessed a keen interest in Japan's rites of laughter in general, and he was especially interested in the *okoze* rite. Surprisingly, Yanagita seems to have been unaware of the rite at the Kagarido shrine. He seems to have been unaware, too, of the story of the brag fest between the mountain goddess and the sea god. So the appearance of the lumpfish in rites of mountain laughter was a riddle that baffled Yanagita to the end.

The *okoze* rite that most interested Yanagita was a festival in the hamlet of Yakiyama in what is now Mie Prefecture. Yakiyama lies along the Ise-ji trail, one of the Kumano *kodo* (ancient pilgrimage routes). Kumano is a region that corresponds to the lower portion of the Kii Peninsula. The *kodo* link the three great Kumano shrines of Hongu, Hayatama, and Nachi, at the southern end of the peninsula, to Koyasan, a center of Shingon Buddhism in the mountains in the western part of the peninsula; to Yoshino, a town in the mountains at the center of the peninsula known for its mountain-climbing ascetics; and to Ise-jingu, on the upper east side of the peninsula.

Making the *kodo* pilgrimage to Kumano's shrines has been a Japanese Buddhist tradition for well over a thousand years. And religious ascetics roamed the hills of Kumano on the same routes long before the arrival of Buddhism in Japan. The United Nations Education, Scientific and Cultural Organization (UNESCO) has recognized the historic and cultural importance of the *kodo* pilgrimage routes, adding them in 2004 to its list of World Heritage sites. Japanese eager to secure the World Heritage registration for the *kodo* had established a council for that purpose. And a reference to Yakiyama appears in the first of a series of newsletters that the council began issuing in 2002.

The Yakiyama reference is in a passage reproduced from a 19th-century collection of information about *kodo* travelers entitled *Shokoku tabibito cho* (A record of travelers from different regions). Yakiyama is near the village of Owase, the site of the *okoze* laughter festival at the Kagarido shrine. And the *Shokoku tabibito cho* consists of documents issued between 1836 and 1849 by the village officials to travelers afflicted by illness or injury.

Yakiyama is on an especially arduous stretch of the Ise-ji *kodo*, roughly midway between Ise-jingu and the Kumano shrines. And the Owase village officials provided generous assistance to incapacitated travelers who needed to turn back. They dispatched attendants to accompany the unfortunate pilgrims on their return route and issued documents that requested meals and lodging for the travelers at post stations along the way.

The Yakiyama *okoze* laughter festival takes place on the 8th day of the 11th month of the lunar calendar. That is the day of a festival held widely in Japan in the Edo period (1603–1868) to honor the mountain deity or deities. Yanagita wrote of the festival in a paper titled "Yamagami to okoze" (Mountain gods and lumpfish) and also mentions it in the extended essay "Warai no bungaku no kigen" (The origins of the literature of laughter). He never, however, visited the hamlet. In fact, he confesses in "Yamagami to okoze" to have been unable to even locate Yakiyama on a map.

Yanagita learned what he knew of the Yakiyama laughter festival from a description in the 10-volume collection *Kidan zasshi* (A historical miscellany of remarkable tales) by Miyaoi Yasuo (1797–1858). Miyaoi had studied under the prominent nativist scholar and Shinto theologian Hirata Atsutane (1776–1843). He detailed in his voluminous work hundreds of cultural and historic subjects, of which the Yakiyama laughter festival appealed especially to Yanagita.

In "Warai no bungaku no kigen," Yanagita explains that the Yakiyama festival begins with the village men sitting together on the ground while the women and children look on from the periphery. His description of the proceedings continues as follows:

The festival leader enters with a lumpfish concealed in his jacket [and takes his place in the center of the group]. The attendees face the leader and ask to see the fish.

"No, I won't show it to you because you'll laugh."

"We absolutely won't laugh, so show us the fish."

Following this exchange, the leader exposes the head of the lumpfish through a jacket sleeve, upon which everyone laughs aloud. The leader then withdraws the fish, protesting that the crowd had promised not to laugh. Everyone then begs the leader to please show the fish again, pledging that they really, really won't laugh this time. The leader thereupon offers another peek at the fish, whereupon everyone laughs anew.

This back and forth continues until the leader finally exposes the whole lumpfish and everyone doubles over in laughter. That laughter constitutes a propitious conclusion to the festival. Thus does something that wouldn't ordinarily strike people as especially funny assume a ritualistic humor for eliciting divine laughter.

The piscine holy fool in this narrative is, to ichthyologists, *Inimicus japonicas*. It gets the common name used here from its spectacularly lumpy head. Other names used for the lumpfish in some regions refer to the poisonous spines on its dorsal fin: devil stinger, demon stinger, and scorpion fish.

At Owase's *okoze* laughter festival, laughing at the lumpfish is an effort to appease the god(dess) of the mountains. The participants in Yakiyama's version of the festival are also making an offering of laughter to the mountain deity. We encounter here the fundamentals of laughter. Those fundamentals are especially clear in the exchange between the leader and the audience at the Yakiyama festival.

We laugh hardest and most uncontrollably when we have been trying to suppress the laughter. The more we have been trying to hold it in, the more explosively does it erupt. Thus does the exchange at the Yakiyama festival center on the leader's admonitions not to laugh and on the audience's pledges, repeatedly violated, to comply.

The lumpfish figures in Japan's mountain traditions apart from festivals. Hunters, for example, would carry a dried lumpfish as a good-luck charm—a plea to the mountain deity to bestow ample game. Japanese falconers abided by a similar practice. The naturalist Minakata Kumagusu (1867–1941; pages 161–165) described the practice in the paper "Yamagami okoze uo wo konomu koto" (The mountain deity's fondness for lumpfish).

> A hunter would wrap [a lumpfish] in paper and carry it in his pocket with the wish, "Please provide me promptly with game, and I'll show you a lumpfish." When the hunter caught the game he was seeking, he would expose just a part of the fish—the tail perhaps, or the head. That would whet the mountain deity's desire to see the whole fish. . . . The hunter would make the vow repeatedly, deceiving [the mountain deity] repeatedly, and the bestowal of plentiful game would continue.

We note the resemblance between the role of the lumpfish in the hands of hunters and in the hands of festival leaders. The fish was in both instances a tool for eliciting bounty from the mountain deity. We recall, meanwhile, the tale of the brag fest between the sea god and the mountain goddess. And we recognize that Yanagita was unaware of that tale. Yet we wonder if the legend is truly the origin of the lumpfish tradition or, rather, an after-the-fact embellishment of an older tradition. And we share Yanagita's curiosity about why a sea fish became a staple of mountain lore.

Yanagita frequently turned for scientific guidance to Shirai Kotaro (1863–1932), a pioneering plant pathologist at what is now the University of Tokyo. He reproduces a letter from Shirai in regard to the lumpfish in his paper "Yamagami to okoze." Shirai includes in the letter an extensive list of names by which the lumpfish was known in different parts of Japan. And he provides a description of the fish:

> Similar in shape to the red rockfish [*Sebastes inermis*] and the marbled rockfish [*Sebastiscus marmoratus*], faintly iridescent, with dark stripes of differing widths running from back to belly, the belly featuring faintly iridescent mottling, the head being identical in shape to that of the marbled rockfish, with short spines above the eyes.

"Fishermen in [the Wakayama port of] Yuasa," adds Shirai, "say that when they catch [lumpfish] they slash them and throw them back into the sea, fearing stings [from the poisonous spines]." And he offers two possible reasons as to why hunters used the lumpfish as a lucky charm.

One reason suggested by Shirai is a dialectical name for the lumpfish in Wakayama: *yama-no-kami* (mountain god[dess]). This suggestion begs the question as to the cause-and-effect relationship between the piscine name and the hunters' practice. But if we assume that Shirai had some sort of basis for concluding that the name preceded the practice, we can attribute a certain persuasiveness to this argument.

Shirai's second reason pertains to the lumpfish's prickly anatomy. He speculates that hunters of old have regarded the fish's sharp spines as auspicious analogies for catching game. Shirai suggests that ancient morphological associations might have taken hold in spiritual belief.

Yanagita seems to have been less than satisfied with Shirai's response. He didn't address his correspondent's speculation directly. Instead, he said that he was interested in looking into the different names for the lumpfish. Yanagita possessed a keen interest in parsing cultural and historical background from contemporary names and expressions. And he took a special interest in the name for the lumpfish used in what is now Fukuoka Prefecture, *mikoio*. Phonetically, *miko* corresponds to the word for priestess or shrine maiden. *Io*, meanwhile, could be a dialectical variant of uo, which means fish.

"The evidence is incomplete," acknowledged Yanagita, "but I believe that the lumpfish was a religious totem used by priestesses [of old]." This interpretation of a regional name for the lumpfish might well explain the fish's role in ancient religious ceremonies. But that leaves unanswered the question as to why the lumpfish was chosen for that role in the first place.

Another problem with Yanagita's interpretation: Japanese totemism frequently involved naming tribes or other human constructions after natural phenomena, but it never involved the opposite. Naming a fish after a religious functionary would be inconsistent with known practice.

Inexplicable, meanwhile, is why Yanagita exhibited little interest in the most common Japanese name for the lumpfish, *okoze*, while exercising a keen interest in the fish's less common names. Here was a researcher fascinated with the cultural and historical implications of names. And here was a name that resonated conspicuously with a subject of profound interest to Yanagita. The name *okoze* fairly cries out its homonymy with the term for holy foolery, *oko*. Yet nowhere does Yanagita express any particular interest in the possible connection. He perhaps regarded the connection as so obvious as to require no mention.

The earliest known appearance of *oko*, in the sense of foolish-ness, is in the *Kojiki*, but the etymology of the word is obscure. Modern Japanese includes several derivatives of *oko*, such as *okogamashii* (stupid) and *okozuku* (to act silly). In *okoze* (lump-fish), *ze* would presumably be the suffix for female. *Okoze* would thus mean something like "silly woman." That would be consis-tent with our understanding of the role of priestesses and shrine maidens in holy foolery.

Buying lumpfish was part of celebrating the festival that Japanese held in honor of the mountain deity or deities in the Edo period (1603–1868). That festival took place, as noted, on the 8th day of the 11th month of the lunar calendar. It was espe-cially important to people whose work depended on materials secured in the mountains, such as carpenters, furniture mak-ers, blacksmiths, and iron founders. Those people would pur-chase lumpfish, which they called *yamagami okoze* (mountain god[dess] lumpfish), to place as offerings on altars in their homes and workplaces.

All of the vocations cited involved something more in the eyes of Edo-period Japanese than merely handling mountain materi-als. They provided an organic linkage with the natural world and between it and "the other world." That association with bridg-ing worlds was especially strong in connection with blacksmiths. They handled fire, the child of heaven and earth, and iron, born of the mountains. Their work, people believed, gave them a van-tage that transcended this world.

Blacksmiths also served as intermediaries between the sea and the mountains. They provided fishermen, for example, with fishhooks. The fishhook links the sea and the mountains in the

Japanese tale of the mountain god Yamabiko and the sea god Umihiko. Before the Bronze Age, fishermen crafted their fishhooks from the bones of animals killed in the mountains. So blacksmiths were carrying on a tradition that antedated their trade.

The lumpfish evokes the flames of the blacksmith's forge with its iridescence. And its dorsal spines suggest the blades that blacksmith's hew. The lumpfish figures in sun worship and in offerings to the sun goddess, Amaterasu. That reflects the belief, found in civilizations worldwide, in the magical power of analogs. The Scottish anthropologist Sir James George Frazer (1854–1941) examines that belief in *The Golden Bough*, a work that exercised a powerful influence on Yanagita (pages 61–63, 157–161).

As an autumn rite, the mountain god(dess) festival coincided with a time of thanking the deities for the year's harvest. It was an occasion, too, for making offerings of light—the lumpfish's iridescence—to Amaterasu as her glow ebbed. The lumpfish was thus a medium for reaching out to the deities. It was a bridge, meanwhile, between seasons and between worlds.

The lumpfish is similar in an important respect to other earth-heaven intermediaries that appear in the mythologies of different civilizations. That similarity is in regard to the trait of duality. The intermediaries exhibit duality across diverse extremes, such as sacred and profane, beneficent and destructive, beautiful and ugly. And the lumpfish is unquestionably ugly to the extreme, at least in reference to conventional human notions of beauty. That ugliness served the worried villagers well when the mountain goddess lost the brag fest to the sea god. As we have seen, they invited the resentful goddess to see the comical ugliness of the lumpfish and to join them in laughing at the spectacularly homely sight.

We note a striking parallel between the lumpfish and the goddess Ame-no-uzume. The lumpfish made its way from the sea to the mountains, where it elicited laughter. Ame-no-uzume's name identifies her, meanwhile as a deity of the swirling tides: *uzu* = "vortex"; *me* = "female"; *no* = "of"; *ame* = "heaven."

Why people needed comicality

Frolicsome rites and dramatic productions long served the purpose in European kingdoms of venting public frustration with monarchs. Executing and replacing a weakened monarch was common practice in most regions. That commonly happened, for example, when an upheaval of natural or human origin cast a kingdom into turmoil. And regicide remained prevalent even in the 20th century, most famously Russia, evoking the surging momentum of the Bolsheviks' revolution. Nonetheless, the mortality rate for sitting monarchs appears to have declined sharply in the Middle Ages. And that decline is partly attributable to nonlethal avenues devised by monarchs for venting public frustration.

In *The Golden Bough*, Frazer describes a "softening down" of the earlier practice of killing weakened monarchs. He notes the importance of convincing theatricality in the event.

> In some places the modified form of the old custom of regicide which appears to have prevailed at Babylon has been further softened down. The king still abdicates annually for a short time and his place is filled by a more or less nominal sovereign; but at the close of his short reign the latter is no longer killed, though sometimes a mock execution still survives as a memorial of the time when he was actually put to death.

Frazer proceeds to detail concrete examples from Cambodia, Siam (Thailand), Samarcand (Uzbekistan), Egypt, Morocco, and the United Kingdom.

To take examples. In the month of Méac (February) the king of Cambodia annually abdicated for three days. During this time he performed no act of authority, he did not touch the seals, he did not even receive the revenues which fell due. In his stead there reigned a temporary king called Sdach Méac, that is, King February.

In Siam on the sixth day of the moon in the sixth month (the end of April) a temporary king is appointed, who for three days enjoys the royal prerogatives, the real king remaining shut up in his palace.

On the first day of the sixth month, which was regarded as the beginning of the year, the king and people of Samarcand [Samarkand, Uzbekistan] used to put on new clothes and cut their hair and beards. Then they repaired to a forest near the capital where they shot arrows on horseback for seven days. On the last day the target was a gold coin, and he who hit it had the right to be king for one day.

In Upper Egypt on the first day of the solar year by Coptic reckoning, that is, on the tenth of September, when the Nile has generally reached its highest point, the regular government is suspended for three days and every town chooses its own ruler. This temporary lord wears a sort of tall fool's cap and a long flaxen beard, and is enveloped in a strange mantle. With a wand of office in his hand and attended by men disguised as scribes, executioners, and so forth, he proceeds to the Governor's house. The latter allows himself to be deposed; and the mock king, mounting the throne, holds a tribunal, to the decisions of which even the governor and his officials must bow. After three days the mock king is condemned to death; the envelope or shell in which he was encased is committed to the flames, and from its ashes the Fellah creeps forth.

The Mohammedan students of Fez, in Morocco, are allowed to appoint a sultan of their own, who reigns for a few weeks, and is known as Sultan t-tulba, "the Sultan of the Scribes." This brief authority is put up for auction and knocked down to the highest bidder. It brings some substantial privileges with it, for the holder is freed from taxes thenceforward, and he has the right of asking a favour from the real sultan. That favour is seldom refused; it usually consists in the release of a prisoner. Moreover, the agents of the student-sultan levy fines on the shopkeepers and householders, against whom they trump up various humorous charges. The temporary sultan is surrounded with the pomp of a real court, and parades the streets in state with music and shouting, while a royal umbrella is held over his head.

A custom of annually appointing a mock king for a single day was observed at Lostwithiel in Cornwall down to the sixteenth century. On "little Easter Sunday" the freeholders of the town and manor assembled together, either in person or by their deputies, and one among them, as it fell to his lot by turn, gaily attired and gallantly mounted, with a crown on his head, a sceptre in his hand, and a sword borne before him, rode through the principal street to the church, dutifully attended by all the rest on horseback.

Yanagita perceived a commonality with the above sorts of practices in Japan's tradition of spirits and goblins and the like. He suggested that Japan's one-eyed goblin, for example, is a vestige of an ancient practice of human sacrifice. His findings led him to hypothesize the following practice.

A tribe whose pantheon included a one-eyed god would select a slave to sacrifice as an analog of that deity. The tribe would provide the slave with lavish care until the time came for the sacrifice. At that time, the tribe would poke out one of the eyes of the unfortunate slave and break one of his legs to prevent him from escaping. The ceremony would conclude with the execution.

We gain another perspective on human sacrifice from the French philosopher Georges Bataille (1897–1962). He discusses sacrifice as practiced by the Aztecs of ancient Mexico in *La Part maudite, I: La Consommation* (*The Accursed Share: An Essay on General Economy, Vol. 1: Consumption*). According to Bataille, the Aztecs would choose a victim from among their prisoners of war to serve as an incarnation of a god. They would make the selection a year before the scheduled sacrifice and, as in Yanagita's example, lavish him with luxury. The sacrifice to be would parade through the city like a king, bouquets in hand, and everyone he encountered, regarding him seriously as a godly analog, would bow deferentially. That godly treatment would continue until the inevitable culmination of the divine role-playing.

Origuchi Shinobu (1887–1953; pages 8–9) concluded from his research that numerous societies selected sacrificial victims on the basis of distinctive physical markings or handicaps and symptoms of specified illnesses. Their members regarded those markings,

Las Meninas *(1656), a masterpiece by Diego Velázquez (1599–1660) in which the subjects include a court dwarf*

handicaps, and symptoms as signs from heaven. The individuals in question were, in the eyes of their fellow citizens, vessels of defilement. They were therefore subjects of fear and loathing, of contempt and derision, of avoidance. On the other hand, that they had been singled out by the gods imbued them with the cachet of holiness. Even in their defilement, they wore the gaze of heaven. Here again is the dynamic of dualism at work in the person of holy fools.

We sense a similar duality in the dwarfs, the hunchbacks, and the other possessors of physical deformities who populated the royal courts of old. Several dwarfs appear, for example, in paintings of the Spanish court by Diego Velázquez (1599–1660). The great painter portrays them sympathetically, even affectionately. He invites our attention to the divinity inherent in those regarded as comic on account of physical traits.

Generations of mountain suppliants have similarly attributed a divinity to the homely lumpfish. This fish, in its very ugliness, has born the defilement of the world. The lumpfish's grotesque appearance is, in the prayers of the suppliants, a holy distinction. Here is a piscine sacrifice accompanied by human laughter in the hope of eliciting blessings from the mountain deity.

Laughter has accompanied sacrifice, believed Yanagita, throughout human history. "The practice of serving the greater happiness of a group through sacrifice in the form of having an individual endure being laughed at is something that didn't begin in the Middle Ages" ("Warai no bungaku no kigen").

Sacrificial or otherwise, laughter was long an offering in the cycle of earthly entreaties and heavenly blessings. People made their offerings of laughter in the context of a worldview that posited "this world" and "the other world." That worldview succumbed, however, to the onslaught of science and scientific rationalism. Meanwhile, hamlets and villages coagulated into towns and cities, and the communal spirit of mutual assistance gave way to individualism, further undermining the basis for community offerings of laughter. Ever-higher efficiency became the all-consuming goal in business and in education, leaving ever-less leeway for laughter in the workplace and in the classroom. That left the home as the final redoubt for collective mirth, yet even that bastion is crumbling as family life splinters into individual patterns of activity.

Accompanying changes in patterns of laughter are changes in the roles and social positioning of those devoted to making people laugh: society's holy fools. We have encountered pockets of holy foolery in its traditional forms in the examples cited in this chapter. In the next chapter, we will examine new forms that holy foolery has taken in the course of social evolution.

CHAPTER 4

>—+—‹•›—○—‹•›—+—‹

Laughter Amid the Evolution of Communities

Reprieves from ostracism

Perceptible in the rites and festivals of laughter described in the previous chapter are vestiges of the supernatural power that people once associated with sound. Through peals of laughter, the participants in those gatherings seek the goodwill of their deities while reaffirming communal bonds. Their laughter thus functions both as sacred chorus and as earthly discourse.

Japanese traditionally credited local deities for the birth and development of their communities. An awareness of those deities figured in every aspect of the life of the communities. Along with honoring the local deities, villagers abided rigorously, according to Yanagita Kunio (1875–1962), by dualistic behavior patterns that corresponded to the ordinary (*ke*) and the special (*hare*), the unaffected and the ceremonial, the informal and the formal, the earthly and the sacred. They exhibited polar extremes of speech, apparel, and mannerisms, Yanagita found, in the alternating phases of village life.

Most villagers adhered to the dualistic behavior patterns identified by Yanagita and abided faithfully by their villages' rules of conduct. Serious transgressions earned a punishment known as *murahachibu* for the transgressors and their families. That term literally means village (*mura*) eight (*hachi*) parts (*bu*). It is in reference to 8 of the 10 kinds of activities that were fundamental to village life and that the villagers undertook communally: funerals, firefighting, coming-of-age ceremonies, weddings, births, medical treatment, home building and renovation, flood relief, annual memorial services for deceased relatives, and travel support.

Murahachibu ostracism entailed withholding assistance in regard to 8 of the foregoing activities—all except funerals and firefighting. Communal assistance with funerals continued because disposing of corpses properly was important for village sanitation and presumably because of a shared concern with appeasing the spirits of the dead. Similarly, firefighting assistance continued even for transgressors because of the common interest in preventing fires from spreading.

Ostracism was a more severe punishment than the occidental reader might suspect from the foregoing description. Interaction with neighbors was central to people's lives, and severing that interaction was tantamount to exile. Numerous villages in western Japan observed a practice that allowed those punished with *murahachibu* to have the ostracism lifted through laughter. The historian Higuchi Kiyoyuki (1909–1997) describes that practice in *Hitozukiai no Nihon-shi* (A Japanese history of human relations).

A transgressor, according to Higuchi, would walk from house to house, escorted by a village official. As the village official struck wood blocks together, the transgressor would recite aloud the details of his or her offense, expressing remorse for disturbing the village harmony, begging for forgiveness, and inviting the villagers to unleash on him or her the humiliation and redemption of laughter. The villagers would gather and comply with a round of hearty laughter, thereby canceling the ostracism and welcoming the transgressor back into the fold.

We hear frequently in Japan that our nation has a long tradition of belief in the redemptive power of laughter. The basis for that assertion, however, is uncertain. Higuchi offers the following interpretation:

> People believed that a person who did a bad thing was not necessarily a bad person. Rather, an evil spirit had overcome the individual, or his or her soul had wavered. Providing spiritual stimulation [through laughter] would rekindle the individual's inherent goodness.

From another perspective, *murahachibu* was the formal manifestation of villagers' anger at neighbors who had threatened their social cohesion. Organized laughter dissolved the anger and thus absolved the wrongdoer. From yet another perspective, Japanese traditionally regarded misdeeds as affronts to the local deities, and setting things right hinged on securing divine forgiveness. Laughter was a means of mollifying the deities and securing absolution for the community.

Holy fools had served Japanese communities since prehistory as mediums for interchange with the gods. The development of structured village societies occasioned more-formal mechanisms for undertaking communication with the local deities. Punishing affronts to the deities with *murahachibu* ostracism was one such mechanism, as was the mirthful process of seeking and obtaining absolution—for the errant individuals and, by extension, for their communities.

Tears and laughter at funerals

Let us take another look at the 10 fundamental activities that Japanese villagers traditionally undertook communally: funerals, firefighting, coming-of-age ceremonies, weddings, births, medical treatment, home building and renovation, flood relief, annual memorial services, and travel support. Let us examine those activities in terms of the dualistic behavior patterns identified by Yanagita: ordinary and special, unaffected and ceremonial, informal and formal, earthly and sacred.

Coming-of-age ceremonies, weddings, births, home building and renovation, and travel were indisputably special and auspicious occasions. Most of these activities were ceremonial, some of them formal, all of them sacred. The other activities among the 10 corresponded to neither of the two categories in Yanagita's basic dichotomy. These are activities that deal with death, fires, sickness, and floods. They correspond instead to a third category, defilement. That category arose, as interpreted by Yanagita, from the atrophy of the ordinary and of the special.

I have reservations here about placing funerals and memorial services in the category of defilement. Those events, especially as conducted traditionally in Japanese villages, are quintessentially formal and ceremonial. People dress up for the ceremonies, albeit in generally subdued tones, and prepare foods, such as red rice (white rice cooked with red beans), that are associated with happy occasions. The affairs would seem to qualify, their subject matter aside, for a more positive categorization.

The death of my father when I was a college student was my initiation to the celebratory character of funerals. On the night of the wake before the next day's funeral service, I was astounded to hear and see my relatives laughing and having a good time. That was my first up-close experience with death and with its associated rites. I had expected a sad and somber atmosphere, and the revelry offended my young sensibility. Only decades later did I realize what a glorious occasion my father's wake had actually been.

Funerals are inherently a bridge between "this world" and "the other world," and laughter has played an important part over the millennia in fulfilling that role. Abe Kinya (1935–2006), a historian known for his work in medieval German studies, examined funeral rites in the West. He had this to say about occidental wakes in the paper "Chusei ni okeru shi" (Death in the Middle Ages), included in the book *Chusei no hoshi no shita de* (Beneath the medieval star):

> Close relatives and friends would gather before the burial for the wake, which was, in the early Middle Ages, a raucous affair. Along with the wining and dining, musicians and jesters performed, and women danced.

Abe concludes that wakes were performances designed for the departed in the interest of consoling their souls.

Tears, of course, will always be part of the funeral experience. Along with the tears that pour forth spontaneously from the eyes of the family members and friends of the deceased, funerals sometimes feature tears provided by people hired or otherwise mobilized for that purpose. China and the Koreas have well-established traditions of well-to-do families augmenting their funerals with paid weepers. We witnessed numerous women weeping on cue at the 2011 funeral of Kim Jong-il (1941–2011), the supreme leader of the Democratic People's Republic of Korea (North Korea).

Yanagita mentions in his 1940 lecture "Teikyu shidan" (A historical review of weeping) the Japanese tradition of hiring women to shed tears at funerals, though he admits to having never witnessed the practice in person. The entry for "weeping women" in my Japanese dictionary cites an example of practitioners of that trade in the Ishikawa Prefecture city of Nanao, and it reports that they charged "by the cup" for the volume of tears that they shed.

We can perhaps regard tears, like laughter, as an offering to the gods, as a bridge between "this world" and "the other world." The ritual aspect of laughter and weeping is ultimately theatrical, and the two constitute the comedic and tragic phases of human experience. Here is how the American sociologist Peter Berger (1929–) places comedy in a historical context and characterizes the equivalence of comedy and tragedy in his book *Redeeming Laughter: The Comic Dimension of Human Experience.*

> Both philosophy and comedy came to bloom in fifth-century BCE Athens. Socrates probably lived from 469 to 399 BCE; Aristophanes's [ca. 446–ca. 386 BCE] first play was performed in 427 BCE. . . . But before comedy was established as a separate dramatic form, it was part of tragic dramas—if you will, it had its own slot within the tragic program. That slot was a so-called satyr play, Dionysian in style, which followed the tragic performances as a kind of postlude. In the most literal sense of that phrase, it provided comic relief. Relief from what? Well, relief precisely from the utmost seriousness of tragedy. After the tears

came laughter. This laughter did not annul or deny the emotions evoked by the tragic spectacle. But presumably it made these emotions more bearable, permitting the spectators to leave the theater and to return to their ordinary pursuits with a modicum of equanimity. Thus the domestication of the comic ecstasy was both psychologically and politically useful.

Analogous to Greek tragedy and comedy are Japan's Noh and Kyogen. Both are highly formalized dramatic forms. Noh tends to unfold in tragic contexts, though happy endings occur occasionally, whereas Kyogen is always comedic. Noh frequently deals with the comings and goings of spirits between "this world" and "the other world." Kyogen invariably deals with secular matters of daily life.

Drama, as a formalized expression of happiness (comedy) or sadness (tragedy), is inherently communal. Weeping or laughing by an actor is an offering to the collective audience, and viewing the performance is a shared experience for the audience members. Similarly, the prayers and wishes expressed by festivalgoers

A Kyogen performance

throughout Japan traditionally evinced a concern with the greater good of the community, rather than merely individual interests. Yanagita discusses that phenomenon as observed at festivals in the Ryukyu Kingdom, today's Okinawa Prefecture. His discussion is in reference to descriptions and commentary in *Ryukyu-koku yurai-ki* (Origins of the Ryukyu nation), compiled in the early 18th century by the Ryukyu government.

> A feature [of the festivals] not to be missed is that each and every one of the wishes expressed by the participants was of a community nature, not a single one being in regard to personal matters. [The wishes] were appeals for such things as peace on earth, food for all, and village security. None touched on such matters as happiness and fulfillment for individual households. People gave praises to the deities, that is, on behalf of the world at large. If all was well with the world, its inhabitants would thrive as one with their heavenly overseers. Spiritual faith and worldly administration merged in support of a socioeconomic framework unique to the islands.

The heritage of laughter bequeathed through folktales

Also demonstrating laughter's communal character are Japan's numerous folktales that feature humorous themes or incidents. Those stories meshed with the dualistic behavior patterns that characterized village life. They served as a vehicle, in other words, for transcending the mundaneness of everyday life and transporting listeners into the world of the extraordinary. That extraordinary world resonates with notions of the special, the ceremonial, the formal, and the sacred, as opposed to the ordinary, the unaffected, the informal, and the earthly.

A doubly extraordinary role for tales humorous or sometimes frightening occurred in a bimonthly rite that became especially popular during the Edo period (1603–1868). Japanese inherited the Chinese calendar system of interlocking cycles of 10 celestial signs and 12 zodiac signs. The etymology of the celestial signs, sometimes characterized as the 10 suns, is obscure and subject to diverse interpretations. The zodiac signs are the 12 animals familiar in the context of "the year of the dragon," etc. Each sign in each cycle coincides with each sign in the other cycle once every 60 days or years.

The 7th sign in the celestial cycle coincides with the 9th sign in the zodiac cycle—the sign of the monkey—on the 57th day (year) of the overall, 60-day (60-year) cycle. Japanese know that day (year) as *koshin*, *ko* referring to the celestial sign and *shin* to the zodiac sign. A belief in Chinese folklore held that three insects in our bodies emerge while we are asleep on the night of that day and report our sins to a deity. The deity in question has varied as peoples of different religious orientations have adopted the belief over the centuries. Whoever the deity, the belief holds that he or she shortens or even terminates the life of the person in accordance with the sins reported. So people developed a tradition of gathering and staying awake all night to prevent the tattletale insects from delivering their reports.

In Japan, people called the nightlong gathering *koshin-machi*, "awaiting the koshin." The participants told stories to each other to stay awake, and that stimulated the development of storytelling, including the telling of humorous tales. Higuchi Kiyoyuki (pages 68–69) suggests in the book *Warai to Nihonjin* (Laughter and the Japanese) that the *koshin-machi* gatherings were important events for reinforcing village solidarity. The practice took hold in the Japanese aristocracy in the Heian period (794–1185) and spread to the warrior class in the Kamakura period (1185–1333). As noted, it became especially popular in the Edo period, when it spread to the general populace.

Edo-period folktales abound, meanwhile, with stories of quick-witted heroes who get the best of tax collectors and other local officials. The protagonists sometimes take advantage of ordinary people, too, but they retain an endearing charm. Most of them have a strong identification with specific locales. The tales of the canny Hikoichi, for instance, center on what is now Kumamoto Prefecture, and those of the equally cunning Kichomu center on today's Oita Prefecture.

Echoing through a millennium of Japanese storytelling is the nation's oldest-known narrative, the 10th-century *Taketori monogatari* (*The Tale of the Bamboo Cutter*). That work, of unknown authorship, incorporates numerous elements from folktales of Japan and, possibly, of other nations. The protagonist, a moon princess by the name of Kaguyahime, and her hapless suitors have elicited laughter from centuries of readers.

Kaguyahime issues an insanely impossible challenge to each of the five noblemen who would have her hand in marriage. The challenges are to bring forth the following items: the stone begging bowl of the historic Buddha, a jeweled branch from the legendary island of Horai, the cloak of a fire rat of Chinese mythology, a varicolored jewel from a dragon's neck, and a cowrie born of a swallow. All five of the suitors prove comically unsuccessful. Three resort to deception and submit fakes, which Kaguyahime sees through immediately. One abandons the quest in the face of adversity at sea. And the fifth fails in his quest on account of death or, in some versions of the story, serious injury.

Japan's Heian-period literature includes several highly regarded novels that feature memorably hilarious scenes. Three examples of special note are *Torikaebaya monogatari* (*The Changelings* or, literally, "If only I could change them!"); *Ochikubo monogatari* (*The Tale of the Lady Ochikubo*); and *Konjaku monogatari* (*Tales of Days Gone By* or, literally, "Once-upon-a-time tales").

Torikaebaya monogatari is about a brother and sister who grow up in reversed-gender identities on account of a curse. That occasions scenes of bedroom farce and other comedy as the cross-dressing siblings grow up, take part in court life, and enter into romantic relationships. The lifting of the curse allows them to revert to gender roles consistent with their physical attributes.

Ochikubo monogatari is a Cinderella-like story of a girl abused by a cruel stepmother. The girl meets and marries a handsome man of high standing and lives happily ever after (while the husband takes revenge on his wife's former tormentors).

Konjaku monogatari, meanwhile, is a massive collection of more than 1,000 stories of Indian, Chinese, and Japanese origin. *Torikaebaya monogatari*, *Ochikubo monogatari*, and *Konjaku monogatari* are, like *Taketori monogatari*, of unknown authorship, and all three have been hugely influential in the development of Japanese literature. We know, for example, that Murasaki Shikibu (late 10th century–early 11th century), the author of *Genji monogatari* (*The Tale of Genji*), read and enjoyed *Taketori monogatari* and *Ochikubo monogatari*.

Yanagita explored the world of Japanese folktales in depth in his monumental *Momotaro no tanjo* (The birth of Momotaro). He penned that work in 1933, 10 years after returning from two years in Europe at the League of Nations.

Momotaro is in some respects the male counterpart of *Taketori monogatari*'s Kaguyahime. Both grow up under the loving care of childless elderly couples who find them in curious circumstances. The old bamboo cutter discovers Kaguyahime at the glowing base of a stalk of bamboo. Momotaro enters into the lives of his guardians after emerging from a peach (*momo* being the Japanese word for peach, and *taro* being a common suffix on Japanese boys' given names). Kaguyahime and Momotaro both mature prodigiously fast: the former into a woman of such beauty that her reputation spreads rapidly throughout the land; the latter into a small but Herculean hero who, accompanied by a loyal dog, monkey, and pheasant, vanquishes demons with feats of strength. Both are models, meanwhile, of parental piety.

In *Momotaro no tanjo*, Yanagita identifies a common thread among European and Asian tales of heroes. He notes that the subjects of a large number of those tales start out as "undersized weaklings" who tend to be "paupers and losers or to possess at least the appearance of a manifest foolishness." These are the sorts of individuals, continues Yanagita, "who go on to accomplish great things [in tales of heroism]."

Let us be alert to a key phrase in Yanagita's observation: "a manifest foolishness." Before the modern era, people in Japan and in other nations tolerated and even welcomed foolery in their heroes. Modernization, at least in Japan, ushered in a preoccupation in schools and in the workplace with seriousness and diligence. Japanese society lost its tolerance for silliness. People came to regard foolery as socially useless, as mere frivolity.

The prodigious little people who populate Japanese folktales are sometimes mischievous, rather than heroic. But those mischief-makers are also an important part of the tradition of holy foolery. Yanagita mentions in *Momotaro no tanjo* the story of *Komekura*.

A man rescues a turtle that is being abused by a malicious boy. The turtle thereupon turns into a beautiful woman and presents the man with a magical mallet. She explains that the hammer will grant any three wishes that the man makes. The man takes the hammer home and asks his wife about what wishes they should make. His wife is long on desire but short on wisdom. She promptly taps the hammer and asks for a thousand servings of millet porridge, which immediately appear. The wife taps the hammer again and asks for a thousand pairs of straw sandals, which also appear immediately.

Now that the couple has a thousand servings of their usual millet gruel, the wife wishes that they could dine, like more-affluent people, on rice. So she taps the hammer a third time and declares her final wish: "*Komekura!*" (*kome* being the Japanese word for "rice" and *kura* the word for "storehouse"). But in a slightly strained bit of punning, *komekura* becomes "small" (*ko*) "blind person" (*mekura*). No sooner has the wife uttered the wish than a thousand little blind men appear who eat the porridge, put on the straw sandals, and run off.

Mekura, incidentally, has given way in polite Japanese to such terms as "visually impaired." So the story of *Komekura* is no more likely than *Little Black Sambo* to appear in future textbooks—surely a step forward in regard to social sensitivity, but a loss, nonetheless, in regard to cultural heritage.

The story of *Komekura* features ever-so-Japanese imagery: a kindness repaid by a grateful animal and rice and sandals. It features, too, imagery common to folktales worldwide: an animal that turns into a person (be it the turtle that becomes a beautiful woman or the frog that becomes a handsome prince); a gift of a magical item (be it a mallet or a genie's lamp); three wishes; and a foolish spouse.

Yanagita's two-year stay in Europe broadened his familiarity with the folklore there. The experience inspired his subsequent research in Japanese folkways. And the international perspective informed his work with a deepened insight into the defining characteristics of Japanese culture.

Mental disorder and laughter

More than 350 million people worldwide suffer symptoms of depression or other mental illness serious enough to affect their lifestyles, according to the World Health Organization. Yet the basis for determining mental illness remains fuzzy and subject to debate. A piquant commentator on that basis was the French philosopher Michel Foucault (1926–1984). He argued in *Histoire de la folie à l'âge classique* (*Madness and Civilization: A History of Insanity in the Age of Reason*) that our determination of mental disorder hinges on historical, social, and environmental factors. The people of each era, insisted Foucault, develop their own definition of mental disorder in accordance with their values.

History records numerous instances of people in earlier eras regarding the possessed, the rapturous, the entranced as seers, as messengers of the gods, as prophets. Most of us today would regard those same individuals, if we met them on the street, as mentally deranged. The Romanian historian of religion Mircea

Eliade (1907–1986) examines the mental orientation of shamans in his *Shamanism: Archaic Techniques of Ecstasy*. Eliade writes that shamans consistently exhibited what modern psychiatrists would diagnose as mental disorders and that their calling was a holy vision consistent with contemporary notions of derangement.

In Japan, lunatics who elicited laughter from their neighbors played an indispensable role in village festivals and ceremonies. Their fellow villagers associated the ability to make people laugh with the ability to bring smiles to the gods. The lunatics exercised a holy foolery that their neighbors valued as a channel of communication with the village deity.

Yanagita writes in "Warai no bungaku no kigen" (The origins of the literature of laughter) that traditional Japanese society valued the deranged giggling of the mentally ajar and assigned important roles to those individuals at religious rites. Crazed children, he writes, were the subject of especially deep reverence. People regarded them as straddling the border between "this world" and "the other world" and as possessing spiritual powers rooted in the latter. Yanagita observes further that a Japanese word for "child," *warawa*, "is the root of *warawayami*, [an intermittent fever] associated with possession by an evil spirit, and has as its root, *warai*, the word for laughter."

Children were guests from the other world, people believed, and the mentally paranormal of any age were individuals who had assimilated the workings of that realm. The crazed utterances of the paranormal thus carried the gravitas of messages from the world beyond. That world was a place where our values and priorities carry no weight, where its messengers displayed a glorious disregard for the money, status, honors, and other things that people pursue so assiduously in this world. Back when people believed in a world beyond, the members of society associated with that world were subjects of respect and reverence. That respect and reverence dissipated, however, when Westernization and modernization extinguished the belief in another world. Instead, people came to regard the paranormal simply as mentally ill or as mere imbeciles.

People also regarded as visitors from the other world the *mare-bito* described by the ethnologist and Japanese literary scholar Origuchi Shinobu (1887–1953). As explained earlier (page 8), Japanese write that term alternately with the homonymic kanji compounds for "visitor" (客人) and "rare person" (稀人), and it refers to deities who paid visits to villages during festivals, groundbreakings for homes, and other auspicious occasions.

Visitation implied travel, noted Origuchi, who adds that "undertaking journeys required a sense of divine mission" in an era when travel was arduous and even dangerous. So the notion of visitation and the accompanying implication of travel evoked powerful imagery. Something that astounded Origuchi was a report by the imperial Japanese authorities about the native people in occupied Taiwan. The report described extended journeys across difficult terrain by spiritually inspired trekkers. "Doing something like that strikes us as mentally unsound," comments Origuchi in a published collection of dialogues with Yanagita, "but their sojourning from village to village was an accepted practice."

Origuchi had posited a cadre of *marebito* deities that brought disruptive elements of the other world to villages and homes through their visits. Yanagita took issue with that hypothesis, insisting that the deities brought order, not disruption, to this world. He presumably believed that any disruption in village communities arose from the internal dynamics of resident holy fools, and not from visitations by external deities.

Yanagita's stance resonates with humorous dialogs in Japan's *manzai* stand-up comedy. The laughs there arise chiefly from mutual misunderstanding between the paired performers. *Manzai* originated in a Heian-period custom of two performers who would walk from house to house and entertain the residents. One, ostensibly serious, would offer a stiffly celebratory New Year's greeting and then dance, while the other, a jester, played a drum. The jester's timing suggested a comical misunderstanding of his partner's meaning. Their presumed miscommunication would elicit laughter from the knowing residents who had gathered to enjoy the performance.

The etymologist Shirakawa Shizuka (1910–2006) elucidates a fascinating connection between misunderstanding and laughter in the kanji for "error." That kanji's modern rendering is 誤. The component on the left, 言, associates the kanji with the act of speech. Our primary concern here is with the component on the right, 呉. The box in the upper part of this component is an element that we encountered earlier (page 7). It is the modern rendering of the hieroglyph ㅂ, for a vessel into which people placed written prayers. Beneath that box is the figure of a person who is dancing excitedly—a Chinese or Japanese whirling dervish—while voicing prayers to the deities. Shirakawa concludes that the kanji for "error," 誤, refers to the misstatement and confusion that tend to arise amid frenzy.

Society's internalization of holy foolery

Scientific rationalism displaced Japan's traditional spirituality as the nation rushed to Westernize and modernize in the late 19th century. Japanese belief in "the other world" ebbed. And Japan's holy fools, who had enjoyed a respected position as intermediaries between that world and "this world," lost their standing. Japanese society's mounting rationalism left no room for Shirakawa's frenzy-induced error. Intolerance for holy foolery locked its purveyors out of the social mainstream. In the worst cases, society literally locked the holy fools away in insane asylums.

Tolerance and intolerance have waxed and waned alternately in the world's civilizations. Where societies have adopted intolerance or abstinence formally in laws and institutions, counterreactions have unfolded through semiformal social machinery. An example is the frenzy of Carnival, which takes place in heavily Catholic societies before the rigorous abstinence of Lent. Catholics, Anglicans, Eastern Orthodox, and some other Christians observe

Rio de Janeiro's Carnival

Lent during the six weeks before Easter with varying degrees of abstinence, such as refraining from eating rich foods, from partaking of alcoholic beverages, and from partying.

A counterreaction to Lenten abstinence has taken shape in the boisterous partying and excesses of Carnival, most famously in Rio de Janeiro. Some have interpreted Carnival as a means of consuming food that would spoil during the Lenten weeks of restraint. Others have suggested that it is a carryover from imperial Rome's Saturnalia and Bacchanalia festivals and even from the Athenian festival of Dionysia.

Carnival was and is a sort of safety valve for releasing pent-up energy, albeit before the fact in regard to Lent. It is similar in that sense to the stratagems employed in several civilizations to defuse popular dissatisfaction with sovereigns. We have seen examples of such stratagems cited by Sir James George Frazer (1854–1941) in *The Golden Bough* (pages 61–63).

"The sudden release of pent-up entropy" is how the cultural anthropologist Yamaguchi Masao (1931–2013) characterized Carnival. "Several societies have incorporated such devices in their cultures, he writes in *Warai to itsudatsu* (Laughter and deviation). "When the time comes, negative energy transforms into creative energy, and the transformative agent is laughter."

Yamaguchi might have mentioned libido, too, as a transformative agent, for the lifting or relaxation of sexual strictures has been part of Carnival in several societies. In that sense, the Carnival tradition calls to mind Japan's *utagaki* festivals. The *utagaki* gatherings are an ancient tradition in Japan and were especially popular in the Nara period (710–794). They took place in advance of the spring planting season and autumn harvest season and evince a strong association with fertility rites. Males and females of all ages would enjoy food and drink together on a hilltop, recite poetry, and wander off in male-female pairs—irrespective of marital ties—for coupling through the night. Poems written at *utagaki* gatherings occupy an important place in the great eighth-century poetry compilation *Manyoshu*.

We note here anew the similarity in the origins of festival traditions in different regions. That similarity is also apparent in the Halloween festivities in several Western nations and Japan's O-bon festival. Halloween takes place on October 31 in conjunction with All Saints' (Hallows') Day. Its costume parties and "trick-or-treat" candy gathering apparently evolved as a counter to the specter of death, which pervades on All Saints' Day.

The Japanese festival, meanwhile, takes place variously in July and August in different regions of the nation. It, too, is a time when people traditionally believed that the spirits of ancestors return home, and families set out lanterns to guide and welcome the spirits. Bon also occasions bon-odori folk dancing, a popular event in towns and neighborhoods nationwide.

O-bon's "O" is a prefix of familiarity, and "bon" is an abbreviation of the Japanese rendering (*urabon-e*) of the Sanskrit *ullambana*. The Sanskrit term literally means "hanging upside down," and it denotes suffering. Welcoming home the spirits of ancestors was a way of ameliorating the presumed suffering of the departed.

Yanagita took note of the tradition of refraining from work at Bon. "People were not to do any routine work at O-bon," he wrote in the 1946 book *Senzo no hanashi* (*About Our Ancestors*). "The holiday was more than a respite from labor. It was a time of abstinence."

Bon-odori folk dancing at O-bon

The dead essentially came to life at O-bon as their spirits visited the homes of their descendants. And the living temporarily abandoned some of the basic practices of life. Origuchi wrote in *Bon-odori no hanashi* (About the bon-odori) that O-bon served the dual role of a festival of the dead and a festival of the living.

> People commonly characterize the [O-bon] festival (if we can indeed call it a "festival") as a time when the community welcomes and honors the divine spirits of the departed. People in the Japan of old, however, made no distinction between the souls of the dead and those of the living. The [O-bon] festival was therefore more a matter of spiritual interchange between the living and the dead.

Yanagita acknowledges in *Senzo no hanashi* that the identity of O-bon has changed over the years. But he regards that change as occurring entirely in reference to the subject of death.

> We can be certain that Bon was originally a ritual for ameliorating our fear of death. Somewhat ironically, it has had the effect of deepening our abhor rence of death.

The ethnologist Fujimura Hisakazu (1940–) has studied the Ainu people of Hokkaido extensively, and he discusses their perspective on death in the book *Ainu, kamigami to ikiru hitobito* (The Ainu—people who live with the gods).

> I hear from the Ainu that, in the old days, the death of an elder occasioned a celebration of the long life that he or she had enjoyed. Funerals for people who had enjoyed long lives were celebratory occasions not only in Hokkaido but also in mountain villages of Honshu. . . . This invites speculation that funerals in ancient Japan were cheerful, and not somber, events.

Minakata Kumagusu (1867–1941; pages 161–165) wrote of the inverted symmetry of life and death in a 1931 letter to the painter Iwata Jun-ichi (1900–1945).

> Turn on the light and the darkness dissipates. Turn off the light and the shadows return. In the same way, when the condemned wavers on the brink of death, those in hell look forward to the birth of a new companion, and if the person regains his or her strength, those in hell bemoan the likely abortion of their realm's prospective birth. When the person finally dies, the family members grieve the loss, and those in hell take delight in the live birth. . . . The [most primitive forms of slime molds] which people disparage as phlegm-like and semifluid are living things, and the more complex forms erected [by slime molds] for launching spores are actually dead material. People see dead material and regard it as a living thing, and they see [what is actually] a living thing and, since it exhibits no [morphological or physiological] specialization, dismiss the primitive form as essentially nonliving material. That sort of misinterpretation by people [is lamentable].

In the inversion sketched by Minakata, death in this world is life in the other world and vice versa. That sense of inversion retains a strong hold on the Japanese psyche. Witness the continuing funeral practice (when the corpse is dressed in traditional

Japanese garb) of wrapping the flaps of the kimono right over left, instead of the standard left-over-right arrangement.

Holy fools mediated the opposites of Minakata's inversion in an era when people believed consciously and literally in the other world. The end of general belief in the other world robbed the holy fools of their standing, as noted, and left a gaping hole in the Japanese sensibility. A powerful sense of the other world persisted, however, despite the outward denial of that world that accompanied modernization.

Rituals like the Bon festival have satisfied an enduring spiritual appetite for interaction with the other world. They have served that appetite surreptitiously in the guise of "traditional customs" and have thus avoided overtly challenging the prevailing ethos of modernization and Westernization.

Social stratification

The emergence of a large middle class of merchants and artisans in the Edo period and the subsequent Westernization of the Meiji period (1868–1912) resulted in the commoditization of Japanese life. Privatization and nascent capitalism shifted community relations to an increasingly economic basis. Meanwhile, the sacred rites that had underlain the spirituality of communal village life became secular amusements. Laughter as sacred rite became laughter as secular entertainment.

Origuchi characterizes festivals in "Nihon geinoshi rokko" (Six lectures on the history of Japanese entertainment) as parties where the guests were deities. In the communal era, the ritual interchange with deities took place at village shrines and at other village commons. And the wishes expressed by the community members were for the greater good of the community at large. We have seen an example cited by Yanagita in what is now Okinawa Prefecture (page 74). "Each and every one of the wishes expressed by the participants," marvels Yanagita, "was of a community nature, not a single one being in regard to personal matters."

In the era of growing private wealth and broadening differentials of wealth, the wishes expressed were increasingly private in nature, increasingly unconcerned with broader community interests. And affluent members of the community increasingly conducted rites for reaching out to the deities in the premises of their own homes.

A continuing concern with maintaining communication with the deities might seem inconsistent with Japan's escalating secularism. This is presumably an application of Pascal's Wager. The French philosopher Blaise Pascal (1623–1662) famously argued that a rational person would live and act as if a god exists. He argued that, if a god exists, the benefit of believing is infinite and the loss associated with not believing is also infinite, whereas, if a god does not exist, the loss or benefit of believing or not believing is inconsequential.

The philosopher Tsurumi Shunsuke (1922–) traces the roots of modern entertainment to private parties that were essentially privatized festivals. He describes the proceedings in *Tayu saizo den—manzai wo tsuranuku mono* (The straight-man/funny guy heritage—purveyors of *manzai*).

> Big parties were scenes of a spirited give-and-take between
> deities who had come from above and those who were resident
> in the community and between people who had traveled from
> afar and the members of the household. On hand to lubricate
> the proceedings were various performers. . . . On the arrival
> of the deities from above, [the performers] repeated phrases
> (believed to have been) bestowed on the longtime residents of
> the community, and [performers] deployed to field those phrases
> replied in kind.

Community festivals were events of universal participation by all the members of the communities. The privatization of festival rites in the form of hosted parties produced a stratification along the lines of participants (invited guests) and spectators (uninvited guests). The latter caught such glimpses of the entertainment as they could from their vantage on the outside looking in. Origuchi suggests in "Nihon geinoshi rokko" that this was the origin of commercial entertainment.

Japanese society, of course, had always exhibited a pronounced stratification, and that was more than evident in the nation's festivals. We read in such Heian-period literature as *Genji monogatari* (*The Tale of Genji*), for example, of mountain dwellers peeking at festivals from behind boulders. The woodcutters certainly didn't participate in the same festivals that Genji did. Modernization, however, produced stratification inside community units where a sense of socioeconomic solidarity had formerly prevailed.

The broadening of wealth and income disparities along new axes of economic functionality occasioned stratification in the pantheon of deities as well as in the human community. Seats at the best parties in town were by invitation only, even for gods and goddesses. Japan's new stratification carved up community mirth, too. The laughter formerly shared among people and their deities as part of religious rites became a commodity elicited by hired entertainers. And that meant a demotion of sorts for the nation's holy fools.

Japan's holy fools had inherited the role of *amanojaku*: little ogres that defy the Buddhist precepts and get punished for their temerity by superior deities. *Amanojaku* embody the temptations that lure humans into inappropriate behavior. Prototypes of the *amanojaku* appear as male and female deities in the eighth-century histories of Japan, the *Kojiki* (*Records of Ancient Matters*) and the *Nihon shoki* (*Chronicles of Japan*). Holy fools long asserted an *amanojaku*-like feistiness in fulfilling their roles in religious rites. The commercialization of laughter relegated the holy fools to such harmless roles as funny-guy counterparts to straight men in *manzai* stand-up comedy.

CHAPTER 5

Urbanization and Modernization

Laughter domesticated

Transforming laughter from a spiritual medium for religious rites into a vocational tool for professional entertainment sheared mirth of its magic. People had relied on laughter to secure the goodwill of their deities and to secure the lifting of social ostracism. Holy foolery waned, however, as modernization, Westernization, and—equally decisive—urbanization purged society of nonscientific beliefs, which came to be regarded as superstition.

The Japanese don't appear to have had a word for superstition, by the way, until the Meiji period (1868–1912). The modernizers of that era, epitomized by the philosopher and educator Inoue Enryo (1858–1919), coined the term *meishin* (deluded belief) for their purposes. They needed it, apparently, to contrast their self-styled enlightenment with what they were portraying as Japan's backward past. Inoue, to be fair, was respectful of Japan's cultural heritage, but he believed that grafting Western thought onto that heritage was essential for national progress.

Japanese economic society essentially co-opted holy foolery by folding the practice of eliciting laughter into the realm of professional entertainment. That echoed what had occurred earlier in the West. Aristotle (384–322 BCE) wrote in the *Poetics* that comedy arose from the song and dance of *komos*, "ritualized drunken processions." Notorious for their *komos* and wild gatherings were the followers of Dionysus, the god of drinking.

Drunken Dionysians reportedly once stormed into a somber ceremony being held by followers of Apollo, the god of light and of moderation, at a temple in Delphi. They sang in loud voices and generally made a huge commotion, disrupting the ceremony horribly. The wise Apollonian priests, however, handled the disruption skillfully. Rather than driving the miscreants out of the temple, the priests invited them to take part in the ceremony through their singing. The priests effectively co-opted the disruptive Dionysians by absorbing them into the Apollonian liturgy.

History is replete with examples of co-opting laughter in the manner of the Japanese and the ancient Greeks. Holy foolery is potentially revolutionary in that it pays little heed to political authority. Those who would rule and secure obedience from a population are therefore wary of unrestrained laughter. Simply forbidding laughter is unviable, of course, so those in power adopt for their own ends laughter formerly intended for entirely different purposes. They essentially domesticate holy foolery and thereby prevent it from undermining their authority.

As holy fools lost their place in the official structures of society, they and their successors became itinerant jesters. Among the peripatetic clowns in the West were former monks who had been tossed out of monasteries for their idiosyncrasies or who had left on their own accord. Japan's jesters included former low-level officials and other individuals of even lower social standing. A lot of the jesters, whatever their background, were individuals eager to pursue freer lifestyles on the fringes of society. They needed to survive, however, and they frequently secured livelihoods as performers employed by the aristocracy or other elements of the establishment.

Yanagita Kunio (1875–1962) wrote that feudal lords in Japan's Middle Ages employed individuals to serve as confidants and as jesters. Writing in "Warai no bungaku no kigen" (The origins of the literature of laughter), Yanagita reports that every feudal lord employed at least one such confidant-jester.

Historians differ in their definition of Japan's Middle Ages. Some place the beginning of Japan's medieval era as early as the 1160s, in the late Heian period (794–1185), while others opt for the simpler delineation of equating the start of the medieval era with the start of the Kamakura period (1185–1333). Opinion differs across a far-broader chronology in regard to the end of the Japanese Middle Ages. Some historians end the medieval era with the start of the Edo period (1603–1868), and some include that period in the Middle Ages and end the medieval era with the Meiji Restoration, in 1868.

Yanagita refers specifically in his discussion of feudal confidant-jesters to the period of Ashikaga rule, from 1336 to 1573. That period bears the name Muromachi, for the Kyoto district where the third Ashikaga shogun, Ashikaga Yoshimitsu (1358–1408, ruled 1368–1394), built his fortified residence. Yanagita explains that the confidant-jesters of the Muromachi period typically dressed as novice Buddhist monks and sported the -*ami* suffix on their names. Appending *-ami* to names was a common practice among the members of artisan guilds in the Muromachi period. An especially well-known example is Zeami Motokiyo (1363–1443), famed for refining Noh as a dramatic art form. The *-ami* suffix is in reference to the Amitabha (Amida in Japanese) Buddha, and it illustrates the Muromachi practice of using Buddhist imagery as a means of asserting a heightened social status.

The Edo period was a time of rapid urbanization in Japan. Epitomizing that trend was the spectacular growth of the period's namesake city. Edo, now Tokyo, became the political and military capital of Japan when Tokugawa Ieyasu (1543–1616, ruled 1603–1605 [de facto rule to 1616]) became the shogun and

Tokugawa Ieyasu (1543–1616, ruled
1603–1605 [de facto rule to 1616])
Painting by Kano Tanyu (1602–1674)

established his seat of government there. Its population swelled to more than one million in the 18th century, making it the biggest city in the world. The Meiji Restoration brought the emperor to Edo from Kyoto, and Edo thus became the imperial capital, as well as the political and military capital. That occasioned the name change to Tokyo, which means eastern capital. Osaka, meanwhile, remained Japan's commercial capital, and it also grew into a bustling metropolis. Kyoto, too, was a vibrant urban center and, of course, was the imperial capital until the Meiji Restoration.

Urbanization produced a large middle class of merchants and artisans, which presented growing demand for entertainment. By the 1670s, forebears of today's *rakugo* comedic storytellers had begun to ply their trade in Kyoto's thriving Shijo-Kawaramachi and Kitano-Temmangu districts. Among them was Tsuyu no Gorobe-e (1643–around 1703), revered as an originator of Kyoto *rakugo*. Another important *rakugo* performer of the late 17th and early 18th centuries was Yonezawa Hikohachi (birth and death dates unknown). He gained a large following with his performances at Ikukunitama-jinja shrine, in Osaka's Tennoji district. Both of the performers cited here made their livings by eliciting laughter through *rakugo*, and we can regard that as evidence that entertainment had become by their time a viable vocation.

The outdoor markets convened periodically on the grounds of large shrines and temples were a favored venue for the early *rakugo* performers. That was in keeping with the ancient tradition of making offerings of laughter to the deities. Whatever the performers earned for their comedy was what the listeners paid in the spirit of religious offerings. Urbanization was a highly secularizing force, however, and *rakugo* became a form of purely commercial entertainment as the Edo period progressed. In Japan's increasingly market-oriented society, the *rakugo* performers were producers of the commodity of laughter, and their audiences were consumers of that commodity. *Rakugo*'s commoditized laughter was a far cry from the spiritual mirth of holy foolery. The domestication of the latter was nearly complete.

Lies and holy foolery

The Portuguese Jesuit missionary Luís Fróis (1532–1597) commented in a 1585 treatise on what he perceived as the Japanese tolerance for lying. "With us, to call someone a liar to his face would be a great libel," says Fróis, "The Japanese simply laugh it off as gallantry." Fróis also witnessed a flexibility with the truth among Japan's Buddhist monks. "Among us, an effort is made to fully keep whatever promises are made to God; the bonzes publicly profess not to eat meat or fish, but almost all of them do so in secret, unless they fear being seen or are unable to."

Fróis lived and proselytized in Japan for about 30 years and became personally acquainted with Japan's leaders, especially the warlord Oda Nobunaga (1534–1582). He was fluent in the Japanese language and was a keen observer of culture and lifestyles. So we can regard him as a credible witness. Fróis appears to have written his treatise as a pedagogical tool for orienting new missionaries and apparently had no plans to publish the work. It bears no title, as such, and we know it by the first line of the

An undated rendering of Luís Fróis (1532–1597) in
conversation with the warlord Oda Nobunaga (1534–
1582) by an anonymous Japanese artist

manuscript: *Tratado em que se contêm muito sucinta e abrevia-*
damente algumas contradições e diferenças de costumes entre a
gente de Europa e esta província de Japão (Treatise containing
in very succinct and abbreviated form some contrasts and differences in the customs of the people of Europe and this province
of Japan).

The treatise comprises 611 couplets that describe differences
between the Japanese and European ways of doing and making
things. Fróis arranged the couplets in 14 chapters devoted to the
subjects of men, women, children, monks, temples, diet, weap-
onry, horses, medicine, writing, homes, ships, entertainment, and
miscellany. His observations are consistently enlightening, and
the subjects that captured the attention of the Jesuit missionary
bring smiles to modern readers.

Sexual mores: "In Europe, the supreme honor and treasure of young women is their chastity and the preservation of their purity. In Japan, women never worry about their virginity. Without it, they lose neither their honor nor their ability to wed." Even defecation posture: "We seated. And they squatting."

Two centuries later, another European bemoaned a perceived Japanese propensity for lying. Sir Rutherford Alcock (1809–1897), the United Kingdom's first diplomatic representative to reside in Japan, served there from 1859 to 1862 and from 1864 to 1865. Alcock was by all accounts a devoted student of Japan, and he was instrumental in fostering British interest in Japanese art. He even became, in 1860, the first non-Asian to climb Mt. Fuji.

Alcock was, in other words, a sympathetic observer of Japanese culture and society. He was astonished, nonetheless, at Japanese notions of probity. His comments about lying appear in a memoir that he penned about his initial stay, *The Capital of the Tycoon: A Narrative of a Three Years' Residence in Japan*.

> A chivalric disdain of life, and readiness to incur death in any shape rather than dishonor, the origin of the *Hara-kiru* [sic], is a striking feature in their character. But it is evidently easier to them to make an incised wound into their stomach than to speak the truth.

"Tycoon," here, refers to the shogun, rather than to business mogul. The Japanese readings are *taikun* and, alternatively and more commonly, *okimi*. It is, along with honcho (*hancho*, "group leader"), one of the few words from Japanese that we have absorbed thoroughly in English—words that, unlike *tsunami* or *manga*, most English speakers use without being conscious of their Japanese origins.

Relativism in regard to truthfulness is a trait observed in numerous societies throughout history. A fun example is the tradition of April Fools' Day, which originated in the West but, like Christmas, Valentine's Day, and Halloween, has taken hold in Japan. The origins of April Fools' Day are obscure. A frequently cited but ultimately unconvincing explanation pertains to the positioning of New Year's.

Nations formerly celebrated New Year's at different dates. France long marked its New Year on the Saturday before Easter. That is a movable date on solar calendars, since Easter's timing hinges on the phases of the moon. But it falls around our April 1. France switched to a January 1 New Year's in 1564 (though it waited another 18 years to switch from the Julian calendar to the Gregorian). The April Fools' explanation in question holds that French opposed to the switch clung to the springtime New Year's and thus earned ridicule as "April fools."

England, however, had adopted the April Fools' tradition of fun fibbing long before it moved its New Year's Day to January 1 in 1752. (The English and Scots formerly began their year on March 25, the date of the Feast of the Annunciation of the Blessed Virgin. Their switch to a January 1 New Year's coincided with their switch to the Gregorian calendar, from the Julian.) Geoffrey Chaucer (1343–1400) refers to the April Fools' tradition, for example, in *The Canterbury Tales*. We thus need to look elsewhere for the origin of the April 1 foolery.

Whatever the origin of April Fools' Day, the day's foolery has found a welcome home in Japan. Japanese newspapers, for example, have developed a tradition of carrying April Fools' articles. Even the staid *Asahi Shimbun*, Japan's most respected daily, has gotten into the act. For example, its April 1, 1998, morning edition reported the invention of a machine for revealing the true meaning behind politicians' obfuscations.

Another memorable April Fools' article appeared in the *Tokyo Shimbun* in 2012, a year after the Great East Japan Earthquake and the ensuing disaster at the Fukushima Daiichi Nuclear Power Plant. That article reported the development of an "anger-fired electric generation system." The system taps the anger of people disgusted with the response to the disaster by the government, Tokyo Electric Power Company, and myriad clueless "experts." According to the article, a group of angry citizens who join hands can generate enough electricity to power a home air conditioner. Let us take heart at the readiness of newspapers to put away their seriousness for a day. That is a gratifying sign that society retains at least some of the spirit of holy foolery.

Yanagita, too, was amenable to having fun with the truth. He relates in the essay "Uso to kodomo" (Fibs and children) a shopping trip by his little brother. The brother, then three years old, volunteered to go buy some fried tofu for their mother. When the brother returned, a third of the tofu had been bitten off. The brother explained innocently that a mouse had jumped out and chomped off a piece. "Our mother, ordinarily stern, couldn't help laughing." Yanagita admitted in *Kokyo nanajunen* (Seventy years of hometowns) to some stretching of the truth on his own account. "I [also] found myself resorting to some poetic license and perhaps a bit of exaggeration in the name of entertaining my parents."

Exaggeration resounds, of course, through generations of folktales. When either the ordinary or the special atrophied, people faced the terror of defilement. They spun extraordinary tales of heroism to fend off the terror and put their minds at ease.

Modernization's rejection of fabrication

We have met two pivotal figures in the origin of *rakugo* comedic storytelling: Kyoto's Tsuyu no Gorobe-e and Osaka's Yonezawa Hikohachi (page 97). They are two of a threesome regarded as the chief progenitors of *rakugo*. The third, Shikano Buzaemon (1649–1699), made his name in Edo, though he was born in Osaka. Shikano was a popular *rakugo* storyteller in constant demand at the homes of samurai and wealthy merchants. He also published a collection of his stories, which sold well. Unfortunately, one of the stories was a bit too clever for the author's good.

An illustration of Shikano Buzaemon (1649–1699) included in a book of humorous stories published by Shikano in 1686

A cholera epidemic had broken out in Edo, and a former samurai and a grocer spread the rumor that drinking a concoction of nandina berries and dried *ume* (Japanese apricot) would prevent the disease. They reinforced the formula's veracity, incredibly, by attributing its source to a talking horse. Their hoax sparked a multifold surge in the prices for both ingredients. And they profited handsomely by selling a pamphlet that described the miraculous formula. The authorities were not amused, however, and arrested both of the hoaxers, executing one and exiling the other.

Under interrogation, the defendants claimed that they had gotten the idea for the hoax from one of Shikano's published stories. That was enough to earn Shikano a six-year banishment to the island of Oshima, south of Tokyo. He died soon after returning to Edo on completing the term.

The shogunate emphasized the qualities of frugality and uprightness, especially in society's samurai class. The authorities took a dim view of samurai hosting lavish parties that featured comic storytellers and other entertainment. They surely welcomed the opportunity presented by the "from-the-horse's-mouth" hoax to make an example of Shikano. His conviction and banishment coincided with the beginning of decades of official suppression of *rakugo* performances in Edo. And the social remnants of holy foolery would undergo even more stifling suppression in the Meiji period's headlong modernization.

Japan's approach to modernization entailed standardizing practices and values across the nation's social and industrial landscape. Standardization requires integrated control mechanisms, and Japan administered its modernization and the accompanying standardization almost exclusively through Tokyo. The novelist Shiba Ryotaro (1923–1996) comments on Tokyo's central role in Japan's modernization push in the Meiji period: "An interesting feature of the Meiji period is the way the capital, Tokyo, became like a distribution point for disseminating [elements of] Western civilization in Japan." This quotation is from an essay, *"Sanshiro no Meiji zo"* (literally, *Sanshiro*'s Meiji tableau), about a novel by the hugely influential Meiji-period author Natsume Soseki (1867–1916). In that novel, Soseki famously sketches the coming of age of a country-bred young man, Sanshiro, who is attending Tokyo Imperial University (today's University of Tokyo).

Tokyo Imperial University was the chief staging point for Japan's sweeping modernization. Faculty members there determined how best to adapt the imports to Japan's needs. Government ministries, staffed with Tokyo Imperial University graduates, then conveyed the intellectual property, along with the university's instructions, to manufacturers, local government offices, and schools throughout the nation. This was the intensely serious business of nation building. Those in charge were even less tolerant of hoaxes or frivolity than their Edo-period predecessors had been.

Scams and hoaxes retained a welcome place, however, in the world of Kyogen, the comical counterpart to the serious drama of Noh. Numerous Kyogen comedies feature a shyster who takes advantage of a simpleton. A well-known example is *Suehirogari*. The root of this word is *suehiro*, which comprises the components *sue*, for "end," and *hiro*, for "broad," and means "fan" (in reference to a fan's outwardly broadening shape). *Suehirogari* is the noun form of the verb for broadening outward. I apologize for trying the reader's patience with this detailed linguistic explanation, but the name and its nuances, as in most Kyogen, are central to the story that unfolds.

The story begins with a master dispatching his servant to town to buy a *suehirogari*. The simple servant doesn't know, however that a *suehirogari* is a fan. He encounters a shyster who foists a used umbrella on him as a "*suehirogari*." The shyster opens the umbrella to demonstrate its *suehiro* broadening. He even teaches the servant a verse and dance to perform in the event that the master is unsatisfied with the purchase. The verse is full of punning on the Japanese word for umbrella and for place-names associated with various deities. We see here the transformation of the mundane (the fan that the master wanted) into the defilement of fraud (the used umbrella foisted on the servant by the shyster) and ultimately into the sacred (as implied by the deities cited in the verse).

The master is predictably angry when the servant returns not with a fan but with an umbrella. Things get hilariously complicated when the servant then recites the verse he learned from the shopkeeper. We would struggle to account logically for the role of that verse in the relations among the characters in *Suehirogari*, but its very absurdity lends a touch of comic elegance to the work.

Kyogen's shysters frequently get caught up directly in the commotion that arises from their hoaxes. That happens, for example, in two Kyogen works, *Busshi* (Buddha carver) and *Roku jizo* (The six Ksitigarbhas), where the shysters impersonate Buddha carvers. In each, the scam involves a person or persons posing as a statue (*Busshi*) or statues (*Roku jizo*) to deceive a prospective buyer.

We encounter a similarly varied and comical cast of characters in the 17th-century collection of funny tales *Seisuisho* (Laughter for curing drowsiness). That hefty work, completed in the 1620s, comprises more than 1,000 funny tales compiled by the monk Anrakuan Sakuden (1554–1642). *Seisuisho*'s colorful array of characters encompasses skinflints, idlers, liars, ignoramuses, braggarts, snobs, simpletons, and numerous other archetypes. Some of the tales are parables in which people come to grief on account of their personal failings, but others are simply fun, like this one about "thunderbolt sushi."

> A fellow in a crowd poses a sudden question to the group. "Have any of you ever eaten thunderbolt sushi?"
> "Nope, never," is the unanimous answer.
> "I figured as much. It's a pretty rare treat," the guy continues.
> "Have you ever had any," inquires a voice from the crowd.
> "Yep. Quite a bit, in fact."
> "What did it taste like?"
> "It was pretty cloudy."

To accuse the teller of this charming tale of "lying" would be churlish. The fibbing here is so obvious, of course, that the teller's intention is clearly to entertain, and not to deceive. Even where the storyteller might actually be pulling the wool over our eyes, we should perhaps be tolerant if he or she has told a good tale and has at least not picked our wallet in the process.

The great American author and humorist Mark Twain (pen name for Samuel Langhorne Clemens; 1835–1910) quipped frequently and famously about the need for flexibility with the truth in storytelling. His biographer Albert Bigelow Paine (1861–1937) had this to say in the prefatory note to the biography:

> Certain happenings as recorded in this work will be found to differ materially from the same incidents and episodes as set down in the writings of Mr. Clemens himself. Mark Twain's spirit

was built of the very fabric of truth, so far as moral intent was concerned, but in his earlier autobiographical writings — and most of his earlier writings were autobiographical — he made no real pretense to accuracy of time, place, or circumstance — seeking, as he said, "only to tell a good story" — while in later years an ever-vivid imagination and a capricious memory made history difficult, even when, as in his so-called Autobiography, his effort was in the direction of fact.

"When I was younger I could remember anything, whether it happened or not," he once said, quaintly, "but I am getting old, and soon I shall remember only the latter."

Cunning fun in the castle and in the countryside

Japanese who would retain a flexibility with the truth amid modernization could draw inspiration from their nation's unifier. Even the cruel and ruthless warlord Toyotomi Hideyoshi (1537–1598) had a soft spot for stories that bent the truth in the name of humor. Hideyoshi, who succeeded Oda Nobunaga (1534–1582) and became the first ruler to unify Japan, had a confidant-jester by the name of Sorori Shinzaemon (birth and death dates unknown). Several anecdotes attributed to Shinzaemon have passed down to us over the generations.

Hideyoshi supposedly had an inferiority complex about his appearance. He once confessed to Shinzaemon that he thought he looked like a monkey. His loyal confidant-jester was ready with a memorable comeback: "No, Sire. So in awe of your greatness are the monkeys that they distort their faces to look like Your Highness's." That reportedly brought a smile to the tyrant's simian countenance.

On another occasion, Shinzaemon reportedly awakened Hideyoshi from a nap. The warlord had snuffed out numerous lives for lesser offenses, so we have to admire this scion of the holy fools for his pluck. "Please wake up, Your Highness. Something incredible is happening. A wood-monger (*ki*: wood; *uri*: seller) is eating another wood-monger!" Hideyoshi was unhappy about being awakened from his afternoon slumber, but he begrudgingly allowed Shinzaemon to lead him to the scene of the unbelievable cannibalism. What awaited them there was the site of a wood-monger chomping on a cucumber (*kiuri*).

Yet another Shinzaemon anecdote is about fun he had with Hideyoshi when the warlord offered him a gift. Hideyoshi had decided to bestow a gift on Shinzaemon and asked the confidant-jester what he wanted. Shinzaemon declined the implicit offer of money and modestly asked for just a grain of rice. "All I would ask of Your Highness is that you double this humble gift daily for a month." Hideyoshi, impressed at his servant's humility, readily agreed to the request—apparently without doing the math carefully.

The initial offering, two grains on day two and four on day three, was still no more than 512 grains after 10 days but had ballooned to 524,288 grains on the 20th day. Hideyoshi, possibly distracted by the responsibilities of ruling a nation, finally realized that he had been duped. At this rate, he'd owe Shinzaemon 536,870,912 grains on the 30th day, and the total for 30 days would be a whopping 450 straw bags of rice (about 27 metric tons). The warlord sheepishly renegotiated the gift.

Shinzaemon's breed of cunning fun also turns up in humorous folktales of Japan. Yanagita and some kindred spirits convened a series of gatherings to study and discuss Japan's tradition of funny folktales centered on quick-witted pranksters. We saw in the previous chapter how different regions of Japan had spawned their own cunning heroes. Yanagita and his collaborators held their gatherings under the name Kichiuemon, a legendary hero in folktales of what is now Oita Prefecture. "Kichi" appears in the names of several canny heroes in regional folktales. We met Kitchomu (the first syllable being an elision of Kichi) in chapter 4. Other regional heroes whose names begin with Kichi are Kichigo, Kichiji, Kijiroku, and Kichinai, as well as Kichiuemon.

Kitchomu got the best of his village headman in a mousy carving contest. The headman was proud of a lifelike carving of a mouse at his house and boasted of the carving to one and all. One day, Kitchomu intimated to the headman that he possessed a mouse figurine that was surely more lifelike than the headman's. This infuriated the headman, who challenged the presumptuous Kitchomu to bring his mouse to the headman's house the next day for a one-on-one comparison. "If yours really is more lifelike than mine, you can have mine to keep."

Of course, Kitchomu didn't really have a figurine of a mouse, but he had a plan. Kitchomu worked all night on a figurine, but what he had come up with by the morning was pretty pathetic. People said it looked more like horse droppings than a mouse. Undeterred, Kichomu carried his creation to the headman's house. The headman was almost beside himself when he witnessed Kitchomu's ever so un-mousely submission, and he dismissed the would-be challenger with little more than a sneer.

Kitchomu, however, was persistent. "The best judge of a mouse," he retorted, "is a cat. Let's have a cat decide which is the more lifelike." He thereupon brought out the headman's own feline to adjudicate the contest. No sooner had Kitchomu put the cat down before the two figurines than the feline leaped onto... Kitchomu's! The canny lad, we learn, had molded his artless mouse from flakes of dried bonito. And he walked away from the contest with the headman's prized mouse figurine.

In another Kitchomu tale, the hero teases the taste buds of an inspector at one of Edo-period Japan's ubiquitous checkpoints. The shogunate established the checkpoints along principal traffic routes, ostensibly to preserve public order. Evoking the threats to "public order" in the eyes of those in power was the phrase "guns in, women out"—to prevent potential usurpers from importing ordnance for the purpose of armed rebellion and to prevent women from escaping their slave-like servitude.

Graft was rife at the checkpoints. The guards routinely lined their pockets with extralegal fees extorted from travelers and quenched their thirsts with *sake* extracted in the same vein. Kitchomu had grown weary of the graft at a checkpoint that he needed to pass occasionally. The guards there would demand a portion of any *sake* that he might be carrying. They would make that demand on the pretense of making sure "that it is what you say it is."

Kitchomu grew so disgusted with the checkpoint guards that he decided to take revenge. When he next passed the checkpoint, a guard asked predictably, "What's in your bottle there?" "Piss!" responded Kitchomu in a sarcastic voice. The guard sensed the sarcasm and said, "Well, let's have a taste to be sure." Kitchomu thereupon removed the *sake* flask packed atop his luggage and handed it over to the guard for the routine extortion. But the guard discovered to his grief that Kitchomu had been truthful about the contents of the flask.

Furious, the guard bellowed at Kitchomu, "Be gone with you and your filthy honesty!" So Kitchomu proceeded on with a payload of *sake* intact. He had buried flasks of the real thing for his and his friends' enjoyment at the bottom of his luggage.

Forgotten but not lost

Japan's purge of holy foolery's legacy was most severe and thorough at the institutions in the forefront of modernization's unifying push: factories, schools, and hospitals. The pursuit of standardization was relentless in products, education, and medical care. Enforcing rigorously unified standards left no room for error, for exaggeration, for misrepresentation, or for fun.

Meiji-period Japanese approached modernization with a religious-like zeal. Only gradually did people begin to notice the limitations of Westernization and its emphasis on minimizing standard deviation. At factories, maximizing profits didn't necessarily go hand in hand with creating products that would capture the imagination of customers. At schools, cookie-cutter education didn't necessarily tap the potential of all students or even of the most promising students. At hospitals, Western approaches to diagnosis and therapy didn't necessarily identify or cure all ills. And the failings of modernization seemed to escalate by the year.

Yanagita was alert to what Japan had lost and was losing. He was determined to record modernization's toll. For Yanagita, holy foolery was an element of Japanese culture that retained the potential to forestall modernization's cultural Götterdämmerung. Holy fools, who shared laughter with no expectation of compensation, were essential to the survival of community spirit.

Of greatest concern to Yanagita were ancestry and home life, deities and spirituality, and rice cultivation and agricultural village culture. Those three pairings were fundamental to his notion of native identity. And they manifested most convincingly, he believed, in the fun and laughter that bubbled forth in festivals and other community interaction. Yanagita perceived in the holy foolery of community life Japanese society's best hope for resisting the juggernaut of modernization. He envisioned a networking of communities independent of the standardization being imposed through Japan's increasingly unified education system. Yanagita sought to build a new framework for education based on the collective wisdom of communities nationwide.

The folklorist Miyamoto Tsuneichi (1907–1981) wrote to Yanagita in response to the latter's call for submissions of folktales to the magazine *Tabi to densetsu* (Travel and legends). That was the beginning of a fruitful relationship of exchange and cooperation between the two.

Miyamoto walked more than 160,000 kilometers through rural Japan, collecting information about village life and culture, about people who chose to live their lives apart from the world of modernization. He described his findings in *Wasurerareta Nihonjin (The Forgotten Japanese: Encounters with Rural Life and Folklore)*. Whereas Yanagita worked from the perspective of recording lost culture, Miyamoto strived to illuminate the living village culture that remained.

Wasurerareta Nihonjin includes a telling episode about Miyamoto's experience in studying a village on the island of Tsushima, in Nagasaki Prefecture. Miyamoto had contacted the village headman about borrowing some historical documents.

The headman was hesitant. He explained that the documents were irreplaceable and that the village had never lent them to anyone for any purpose whatsoever. This was something, the headman said, that would require the approval of the village council. He graciously convened a meeting of the council with an eye to complying with Miyamoto's request.

Miyamoto arrived at the appointed hour on the day of the council meeting. He knew more about village life than to expect a brief or simple conclusion. The comments from each participant would be long-winded. The proceedings would digress repeatedly into seemingly irrelevant territory. The exchanges would be occasionally heated, occasionally comical. The result would be uncertain until the end. The meeting might well drag on for hours.

Hours indeed! In the event, Miyamoto found himself enmeshed in a two-day marathon palaver that offered no breaks for sleep. He had cultivated an ally, however, in the village headman. And the latter's support ultimately carried the day. Miyamoto secured access to the materials he needed and wanted to further his study of the Tsushima Island village.

From the community to the household

Modernization shifted the focus of Japanese society from communal mutual assistance to economic individualism. That trend began during Japan's national seclusion during the Edo period and attained explosive momentum with the Westernization of the Meiji period. It transformed public laughter from a spiritual offering to the deities into a commercial offering to consumers. And it transferred the locus of ritual laughter from public spaces to individual households. Family members inherited the role of the holy fools in their mirthful offerings to the deities of their homes. That occasioned a growing popularity for games played by family members on special occasions, such as New Year's. A good example is the game *Fukuwarai* (Happy laughter).

In playing *Fukuwarai*, we start with a sheet of paper on which is drawn or printed the silhouette of a woman's round face and pieces of paper that bear the facial features. The players take turns positioning the features on the face while blindfolded. No one wins or loses, for the game has no right or wrong and no scoring. Everyone just enjoys laughing at the frequently hilarious results of the blindfolded placement.

We always played *Fukuwarai* at New Year's at my house when I was growing up, and my friends' families all played it, too. The traditional version of the game seems to be less popular than it was in my youth. Virtual versions thrive, however, on the Internet.

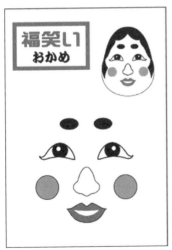 

Everything you need to get started playing Fukuwarai

The history of *Fukuwarai* is unclear. Several sources place the game's origins in the Edo period, but that placement has proved impossible to corroborate definitively. The game does not appear in the monumental *Morisada Manko* encyclopedia of Edo life-styles. Kitagawa Morisada (1810–unknown) compiled that 35-volume, 1,600-entry work in the mid-19th century, and he devoted a whole volume to children's games without mentioning *Fukuwarai*. In the 20th century, Yanagita wrote extensively about children's amusements, and he doesn't mention this game anywhere either.

We find a possible lead in our search for *Fukuwarai*'s origins in a collection of works by Katsushika Hokusai (1760?–1849), the great ukiyo-e artist. Hokusai left thousands of sketches of landscapes, flora and fauna, everyday life, and supernatural subjects that were collected and published in 15 volumes as *Hokusai Manga*. [Note that the *manga* of the title refers simply to sketches. None of the volumes are narratives in the sense of the comic books now known as *manga*.]

Twelve of the volumes appeared during Hokusai's life, starting in 1814, and three appeared posthumously. The 15th and final volume appeared in 1878, nearly 30 years after Hokusai's death, and is of dubious authenticity. That is the volume in which we find a hint as to the beginnings of *Fukuwarai*.

A print in the 15th volume of *Hokusai Manga* portrays Chinese children playing a game that appears strikingly similar to *Fukuwarai*. As noted, the authenticity of the works in the 15th volume is questionable, but whether or not this print is by Hokusai is immaterial here. Someone in the 19th century knew of and rendered in a woodblock print a scene of a possible forebear of *Fukuwarai*. So we can at least hypothesize that the game arrived from China during the Edo period and spread throughout the nation.

Fukuwarai might well have served as a sort of lucky charm for households. People generally spoke in the feminine of the deity of homes. And Edo-period householders were presumably eager to stay on the good side of their protective deity. *Fukuwarai*'s plump face and the ridiculous countenance that resulted from the blindfolded fun would surely have reassured a female deity jealous of potential rivals.

An enabling condition for the popularization of *Fukuwarai* was the emergence of mass-production technology for paper and for color printing. Woodblock prints of popular actors appeared in homes nationwide. And girls enjoyed cutting out the wigs from different prints and putting them on the heads of figures in different prints—a precursor to paper dolls.

Also figuring in the spread of *Fukuwarai* was a practice associated with the yin and yang beliefs imported from China. Among those beliefs was one that life is a sequence of alternating periods of seven years of good fortune and five years of the opposite. A tradition developed of ceremonially gathering seven auspicious items at the beginning of a seven-year cycle of good fortune.

People typically chose items whose names began with the syllable *fu* because that coincided with the first syllable of the word for happiness, *fuku*. That tradition included displaying or sending pictures of a round face that featured seven associations with *fuku*. For example, the hair might be a tassel (*fusa*), the eyebrows brushes (*fude*), the nose rendered with the phonetic character for fu (ふ), the mouth a bag (*fukuro*), and so on.

"To the households of those who smile do blessings accrue."
In the spirit of that old saying, Japanese families developed traditions of household laughter. New Year's was a time of especially
robust laughter, as when playing *Fukuwarai*. The laughter helped
dispense with any inauspicious residue of the old year and usher
in good fortune for the new year or, as in our yin-yang example,
for the next seven years.

Cities' year-round celebration

Urbanization unfolded as a raucous, year-round outpouring of
energy, including an unmodulated flood of entertainment. It was
a round-the-clock celebration that blurred the distinctions that
Japanese society had traditionally made between the ordinary and
the special, the unaffected and the ceremonial, the informal and
the formal, the earthly and the sacred.

Yanagita cited a result of that blurring in his 1931 book *Meiji
Taisho shi—se so* (A history of the Meiji and Taisho [1912–1926]
periods—social trends, published by Asahi Shimbun Company as
the fourth volume in a six-volume series about the history of the
Meiji and Taisho periods). That result was the breakdown of the
rules that had governed who could wear what colors of specified
formal garments. Traditionally, only the emperor, for example,
could wear blue or brownish yellow, only a former emperor red,
the crown prince orange, and top-ranking court officials deep
purple. People avoided wearing outer garments of all white except
at religious ceremonies and funerals.

The taboo on wearing all-white outer garments ended, according to Yanagita, when Japanese adopted white aprons. "One

reason," he wrote, "was that people realized that the differing practices of foreign nations [that Japanese encountered on ending their national isolation] offered benefits and no harm. A bigger reason, however, was the blurring of the distinction between the ordinary and the special. Excitement that people had formerly experienced only on rare occasions gradually became commonplace. Modern-day people have attained a progressive and continuous state of excitement."

In Japanese, the word for "city," *toshi*, is a compound of *capital* and *market*. Cities in most nations grew up around the sites of markets. People held markets in Japan and in numerous other nations only on designated days. Traces of that practice are evident in place-names throughout Japan. The name of the Mie Prefecture city of Yokkaichi, for instance, means "four"-day (*yokka*) market (*ichi* [this being another reading of the same kanji that appears in the compound for *city*]). A market took place there on the 4th, 14th, and 24th days of the month. Markets, which were special occasions, morphed into cities, which were chronic events. That is the process of urbanization that culminated in Yanagita's "continuous state of excitement."

Japanese in olden times chose auspicious sites, such as places where rainbows had arisen, to hold markets. The etymology of the Japanese kanji for *market* suggests a connection with the kanji for *level* and, by extension, with the notion of fairness. A market was a place where goods were to be bought and sold at fair prices.

In markets did the progenitors of *rakugo* comedic storytelling ply their nascent trade. On the market days—special days—did the scions of holy foolery share heavenly inspired laughter with the buyers and sellers. There did they lay a foundation, ironically, for the industry that would domesticate laughter through the cinematic straightjacket of movies, through the insufferable imbecility of television, and through the numbing ubiquity of the Internet.

CHAPTER 6

Globalization

Yamashita Kiyoshi

Japan was, by the dawn of the 20th century, well on the way to unprecedented social and cultural homogenization. That homogenization dissolved, to a great extent, the dynamics of holy foolery. Notable examples of resistance persist, however, throughout the 20th century and into the present century. An especially notable resister was the artist Yamashita Kiyoshi (1922–1971).

Yamashita is famous today for his *chigiri-e* (torn-paper pictures) and for his remarkable life. He was born in Tokyo's Asakusa district but moved with his family to his parents' hometown of Niigata at the age of one. That moved followed the Great Kanto Earthquake, which destroyed the family's Asakusa neighborhood. In Niigata, Yamashita suffered a serious abdominal ailment that left him with a mental disability and a speech impediment.

The family returned to Asakusa in 1926, and Yamashita entered elementary school. His school life was unhappy, however, as his disabilities invited bullying from the other students. Yamashita's

121

home life was unsettled, meanwhile, on account of the death of
his father in 1932, his mother's unhappy second marriage, and
successive moves after his mother fled home with Yamashita and
his two siblings in tow.

Yamashita was unable to keep up with his schoolwork even
after changing schools, so in 1934 his mother enrolled him in the
Yawata Gakuen. The Yawata Gakuen was a school for mentally
disabled children in what is now Chiba Prefecture, just east of
Tokyo. There, Yamashita encountered and displayed an impressive talent for the art of *chigiri-e*, which basically consists of creating collages with pieces of colored paper and can have an effect
remarkably like watercolors.

The school's psychiatrist took note of Yamashita's talent
and helped the youth nurture his artistic potential. *Chigiri-e* by
Yamashita appeared in group exhibitions at Waseda University in
1937 and 1938, and he held his first one-man show in Ginza in

The peripatetic Yamashita Kiyoshi (1922–1971) in his
natural element

1938, followed by another one-man show in Osaka the following year. The exhibitions created a sensation and earned praise from the prominent artist Umehara Ryuzaburo (1888–1986).

Yamashita abruptly took leave of the Yawata Gakuen in 1940. Here is what he later wrote of his flight from the school in a memoir published as *Yamashita Kiyoshi no horo nikki* (Yamashita Kiyoshi's journal of wanderings):

> I had spent six-and-a-half years at the Yawata Gakuen. So I was tired of the place. I wanted to do something different. So I decided to run away. I knew that the teachers would catch me if I did my escape in a dumb way. So I needed to do it right.

For the next three years, Yamashita moved from place to place in Chiba. He survived by doing odd jobs: working at a fish market, at a blacksmith's, at a boxed-lunch shop, as a house servant at a residence maintained by a man for his mistress, and at a restaurant. The 21-year-old Yamashita was working at the restaurant when staff members from the Yawata Gakuen found him there. Japan was at war, and they had Yamashita undergo a mandatory physical and psychological examination for induction into the military.

Military service had been Yamashita's greatest fear. He was therefore hugely relieved when the inspectors found him unfit for service on account of his mental disability.

> That was my worst nightmare, joining the army and getting beaten up by everyone, going to war and seeing scary things, running into the enemy and getting killed. (*Yamashita Kiyoshi no horo nikki*)

Yamashita's second-worst nightmare was getting committed to a mental hospital. That came to pass, however, when he was 28.

Yamashita traveled throughout Japan more or less continuously from 1940 to 1954. His travels took him in 1950 to Kofu, a city about 100 kilometers west of Tokyo. While there, he stripped off his clothes in public at the urging of a crowd. Yamashita pulled the stunt in the sense of jesting, but the police were not in a playful mood. They took him into custody, and the authorities summarily committed him to a mental hospital. For Yamashita, the mental hospital was essentially a jail.

> I could see that they were going to take me to a mental hospital. "Mental hospital" meant the loony farm, and going to the loony farm was the same thing as getting thrown into jail. I wished I hadn't done such a stupid thing. I never dreamed that I would end up getting led away in handcuffs. But it was too late for regrets. They handcuffed me and led me away. This was a disaster. (*Yamashita Kiyoshi no horo nikki*)

A true holy fool, Yamashita discovered humor while confined in the mental hospital.

> The parents of the patients came to visit occasionally. The parents of one patient mentioned Hiroshima, and their son asked if they were talking about an island [*shima*]. Hearing the patients' conversations was sometimes like listening to stand-up comedy. (*Yamashita Kiyoshi no horo nikki*)

Yamashita ultimately found confinement unbearable, its humorous aspects notwithstanding, and he escaped after four months. His guard left him alone in the bath one night to answer the telephone. Yamashita grabbed his clothes and fled, naked and on foot. He ran until he collapsed, but he had succeeded in escaping his prison.

We find a fascinating record of Yamashita's travels throughout Japan in his *Nihon burari burari* (Wandering Japan). That book

Two works by Yamashita

includes an interesting account of a visit to Tokushima to attend an exhibition of his work.

> I felt strange when someone asked me if I was "Mr. Yamashita." An elementary schoolboy then asked, "Hey mister, are you good at pictures." I wasn't sure if I was, so I said, "I don't know." That made everyone laugh. Another kid then asked how to get good at making pictures. That was a difficult question, and I said so. That also made everyone laugh. And I thought it was sort of funny, too.

Another episode in *Nihon burari burari* is about a visit by Yamashita to Nagasaki to attend an exhibition of his work there.

> The Okamasa Department Store [later the Nagasaki Store of Hakata-Daimaru, since closed] in Nagasaki was holding an exhibition of my pictures. I was eating in the cafeteria, and a guy across the table from me was talking to someone and mentioned my name. "There's just hairsbreadth of difference," he said, "between me and Yamashita Kiyoshi." That took me my surprise, since I didn't know that hair could breathe. So I asked the guy about our hair's breath. That made everyone laugh out loud.

In 1961, the psychiatrist who had recognized Yamashita's artistic talent at the Yawata Gakuen took him on a 40-day trip to Europe. Yamashita rendered the sights in numerous works and recorded his impressions in the book *Yoroppa burari burari* (Wandering Europe). Among the humorous episodes in that book is one about a visit to the airline lavatory en route to Europe.

> I was about to burst, and I made a barefoot dash for the lavatories and opened the door of one that was vacant. Two women who take care of the passengers came running and grabbed me and said that I couldn't use that lavatory because it was just for women. So I hurried over to the handle [on a door] on the side of the plane and tried to open it. I really had to go, but the door wouldn't open, so I kept trying with all my might.

One of the women [who took care of the passengers] then shouted for the men who take care of the airplane to come. Two men came and grabbed my arms and said, "This is the door for an emergency exit. If you open it, you'll get sucked out into the sky." I was amazed to hear that and let go [of the handle]. I was so startled that I couldn't pee right away after I finally got into the lavatory. But I finally got the job done and then got some sleep.

Yamashita's work achieved great popularity during his life, which a cerebral hemorrhage ended prematurely at the age of 49. And that popularity proved enduring. He even became the subject of a popular television series that aired from 1980 to 1987.

The challenge of utility

Japanese admire Yamashita Kiyoshi less as a model for modern life than as a nostalgic reminder of the diversity that once prevailed in their nation. The holy foolery exemplified by Yamashita has withered amid modernization and globalization.

Especially onerous among modernization and globalization's tools for crushing diversity and enforcing unified values has been the sop of utility. The German sociologist, philosopher, and political economist Max Weber (1864–1920) and the French philosopher Georges Bataille (1897–1962) insisted that the first people to impute value systematically and, thus, measurably to utility were ascetically diligent businesspersons. Utility subsequently became the driving virtue in the development of capitalism, the transcendental value of utility a truth among truths.

The chief denominator of utility in modern society has been financial currency. "Show me the money!" And nominal utility has multiplied nominal utility tautologically through return on capital. One means of securing return on capital is interest earned on deposits, bonds, and other financial media.

Interest has been the subject of suspicion, regulation, and even outright prohibition in different civilizations throughout history. Jewish authorities imposed restrictions in the pre-Christian era to limit usury. And Christian bishops at the First Council of Nicaea, in 325, enacted a self-imposed prohibition on charging interest in excess of 1 percent annually. Sharia Islamic law, by contrast, continues to forbid charging interest, either fixed or floating, on loans. And that prohibition underlines the sense of "different-ness" that Westerners perceive in Islam.

Western antipathy toward Islam has escalated since the September 11, 2001, terrorist attacks on US targets. The philosopher Nakazawa Shin-ichi (1950–) laments that antipathy in his post-9/11 work *Midori no shihonron* (Green capitalism).

> Islam, by its very existence, is a sort of economic critique [of capitalism]. In principle, Islam constitutes a massive, living volume [that we would rightly know as] *Green Capitalism*. Here, existing undeniably on the earth, is an entity foreign to capitalism. Islam is an indispensable mirror for our world.

Islam's "indispensable mirror for our world" is a looking glass for reflecting on our acceptance of diversity. Differences among political, economic, and religious perspectives have long shaped international relations. And geopolitical delineation entered a new phase with the Communist-capitalist struggle. State capitalism was unforgiving of alternative politico-economic models, and it therefore crushed the Communist upstart.

Only time will tell if Islam's socioeconomic model will withstand the pressures of Westernization and globalization. Peaceful coexistence between Islamic civilization and state-capitalist civilization would be invaluable in maintaining some measure of diversity on the planet. So let us hope that some sort of sustainable accommodation will be forthcoming.

Meanwhile, the challenge of preserving a minimal level of cultural diversity remains a pressing domestic issue for Japan. Among the victims of utilitarianism in Japan has been the nation's formerly rich palette of regional dialects. I recently took in a performance of traditional *manzai* stand-up comedy in which the humor centered on local idioms. The performance was a gratifying reminder that linguistic diversity remains a living—albeit greatly diminished—dynamic of Japanese culture. All in attendance surely came away with a heightened sense of urgency about the need for honoring our linguistic heritage.

A striking voice for preserving Japan's linguistic diversity is that of Ishimure Michiko (1927–). Ishimure is the author of a gripping account of the tragic Minamata environmental disaster, *Kukai jodo—waga Minamatabyo (Paradise in the Sea of Sorrow—Our Minamata Disease)*. That disaster resulted from the discharge of methylmercury-tainted effluent from a chemical plant operated by the company now known as Chisso Corporation. The tragedy takes its name from the site of the plant, the Kumamoto Prefecture city of Minamata. There, the discharge of tainted effluent into Minamata Bay continued from 1932 to 1968.

People and animals that ate mercury-contaminated fish and shellfish from the bay developed such symptoms as brain damage, physical deformities, numbness, involuntary movements, loss of consciousness, and death. Physicians began noting the symptoms of Minamata disease in 1953, but not for another 15 years did researchers discover the link to mercury contamination.

Ishimure described her interaction with the victims of the mercury contamination in a newspaper interview. In that interview, she emphasized the crucial role of regional dialect in expressing the suffering and accompanying compassion. Ishimure identified a stance in Minamata that transcended utility in conveying something essentially human directly through the local idiom.

> As far as I could tell, the . . . ethical capacity for human empathy resided in the world of pure dialect. Translating thoughts into standard Japanese would have purged them of the emotion from which they sprang. Words are indispensable in expressing the [feelings of the] heart. And dialect is indispensable [in conveying the spirit behind the words].

The comments by Ishimure about the straight-from-the-heart purity of the vernacular call to mind the work of St. Francis of Assisi (1181 or 1182–1226). St. Francis was wary of the extensive reliance on Latin in the Catholic church. His heartfelt belief was that everyone should be able to communicate with God in his or her own language. And he frequently employed the Umbrian dialect in his writings, rather than Latin.

St. Francis is famous for his love of animals, as well as for his ability to convey the teachings of Jesus to one and all. Both of those facets of his persona figure in a beloved story about him preaching to birds. While traveling through Italy's Spoleto Valley with a group of companions, Francis spied a great gathering of birds of all kinds and ran into the woods to see them more closely. He had expected the birds to fly off on his approach, but they all stayed in place as if to hear what he had to say.

St. Francis Preaching to the Birds
Fresco by Giotto di Bondone (1266–1337),
started in 1297 and completed in 1299

Francis thereupon shared the message of Jesus with the winged
host. He reminded the birds that they had their Creator to thank
for their plumage, for their ability to fly, and for the sustenance
provided them by their environment. The feathered listeners
were attentive to the end, when Francis walked among them,
caressing each with his tunic and blessing them all. This parable has inspired numerous artistic renderings over the centuries.
Especially impressive and well known is a fresco by Giotto di
Bondone (1266–1337) in the Upper Church of San Francesco in
Assisi, Italy.

Germany's scatological prankster and Hollywood's comic geniuses

The nation most strongly associated with the pursuit of practical utility has also spawned a surprising amount of holy foolery. Epitomizing German holy foolery is the irrepressible prankster Till Eulenspiegel. Till is familiar to classical music audiences worldwide as the protagonist of the popular tone poem by Richard Strauss (1864–1949) *Till Eulenspiegels lustige Streiche* (*Till Eulenspiegel's Merry Pranks*).

Tales of Till arose in German folklore in the Middle Ages. Something of an antihero, Till turns the tables on the greedy and the hypocritical. His pranks frequently leave the unwitting victims with, well, shit on their faces. Scatological episodes abound. Till passes off lumps of excrement as "fruits of the tree of prophecy," sells a frozen concoction of egesta as animal fat, smears feces on a pharmacist's medicine vials, scatters the like on a cart of plums and on a tradesman's animal skins, and otherwise decorates the world about him with the odiferous matter.

The scatology in the tales of Till echoes the violent mischief wrought in Japanese mythology by Susa-no-o in the realm of his sister, Amaterasu (pages 171–172). Even the name Eulenspiegel might have a Japanese doppelganger. One etymological theory is that the name arose from the Low German *ul'n Spegel*, which means "wipe the arse." Similarly, some Japanese scholars trace the linguistic origins of *oko-no-mono* (holy fool) to a term for feces.

Germany's Till Eulenspiegel differs in an important respect from the other European examples of holy fools that we have examined. Our European examples have centered on insiders; for example, comic stand-ins for the sovereign in nonlethal burlesques on regicide and dwarfs and other physically deformed individuals who served in imperial courts. Till, however, was the consummate outsider—a thorn, not an ointment, in the side of the moneyed and the powerful.

The United States, meanwhile, has been fully the equal of Germany in pursuing utility to the extreme, whether in the conveyor assembly line refined by Henry Ford (1863–1947) or in the General Electric supercharged by Jack Welch (1935–). US utilitarianism has elicited diverse counterreaction, a lot of it energized with the spirit of holy foolery. That energy has boiled over onto the silver screen, as in some classic comedies of the depression era.

An immortal send-up of the obsessive pursuit of utility through mechanization is the 1936 film *Modern Times*, written, directed, and scored by and starring Charlie Chaplin (1889–1977). The very efficiency of industrialization, in Chaplin's analysis, was responsible for the unemployment and privation of the Great Depression. And Chaplin's protagonist in *Modern Times* stumbles through one misadventure after another in a comically

Charlie Chaplin (1889–1977) in Modern Times *(1936)*

dehumanizing factory. He and his romantic counterpart ultimately leave the world of insanely utilitarian industry behind and walk off into the sunset, two holy fools eyeing a better life. "Buck up—never say die!" smiles the Chaplin character reassuringly in the closing scene. "We'll get along."

Another holy fool of early cinema was the onscreen persona created by the inimitable Buster Keaton (1895–1966) in silent films and later in talkies. Underlying the holy foolery was the actor's spectacularly physical comedy. Keaton, known as the Great Stone Face for his characters' deadpan demeanor, performed daring stunt work on his own. The stunts were frequently in connection with the protagonist extracting himself from some sort of predicament, and the act of fleeing became an allegory for escape from the absurdities of contemporary society.

Absurdity was a recurring theme in US film comedy of the 1930s, presumably reflecting people's disillusionment born of the depression. Paragons of the absurd in onscreen comedy were the Marx Brothers, a comedy team popular in the first half of the 20th century. But bizarre twists of logic also colored the humor of such comedic screen icons as W. C. Fields (1880–1946).

The *heyoka* jesters of the Great Plains

While we are taking a look at North America, let us note that the continent's tradition of holy foolery predates cinema and even the arrival of Europeans. Holy foolery was part and parcel of the job description of those responsible for healing and soothing in numerous tribes of Native Americans. In English, we have long since adopted the term medicine men (women) for those individuals. But let us bear in mind that their work transcended conventional Western notions of diagnosis, treatment, and pharmacology. The medicine man or woman in a lot of tribes was the quintessential holy fool: an individual who was believed to be capable of mediating between people and their deities and who sometimes played the role of the jester in exercising that capability.

Heyoka is the term used by the Lakota Sioux, of present-day North Dakota and South Dakota, for medicine man or woman. Below is a slightly edited excerpt from the Wikipedia entry for *heyoka*. The Lakota were a powerful tribe in the Sioux nation, and *heyoka* were a powerful influence in Lakota life.

> Among the Lakota people, the *heyoka* was a contrarian, jester, satirist, or sacred clown. The heyoka spoke, moved and reacted in an opposite fashion to the people around them. Only those having visions of the thunder beings of the west, the Wakinyan, could act as *heyoka*.

The most famous and powerful Lakota of all, Tatanka Iyotake (Buffalo Bull Sits Down = Sitting Bull; c. 1831–1890), was a medicine man, as well as a chief. Sitting Bull famously shaped and inspired a large coalition of Sioux, Cheyenne, and Arapaho in the 1870s. In 1876, warriors of that coalition annihilated five cavalry companies led by Lieutenant Colonel George Armstrong Custer (1839–1876) at the Battle of the Little Bighorn in present-day Montana. The warriors went into battle fortified with a vision that Sitting Bull had seen of his people dispatching US soldiers.

Sitting Bull, like a lot of the members of Native American tribes of the Great Plains, engaged in the Sun Dance ritual. The details

The great heyoka *and chief Tatanka
Iyotake (Sitting Bull; c. 1831–1890)*

of the dancing varied among tribes, and those most familiar
with the ritual have always been loathe to share its secrets. The
limited information available suggests, however, that the Sun
Dance could be a grueling ordeal, sometimes complete with body
piercing.

The social anthropologist Abe Juri witnessed a modern holding of the Lakota Sun Dance. She described the event in *Amerika
senjumin no seishin sekai* (The spiritual world of the American
indigenous peoples).

On the third day of the Sun Dance, the *heyoka* appears. By that day, the Sun Dancers are approaching their physical limits. I heard repeatedly that the third day is the most excruciating, that it is the make-or-break day for the dancers. When the *heyoka* appears, he brings a bucket filled with water and a ladle. He stops in turn before each of the Sun Dancers, scoops a ladleful of water out of the bucket, and drinks it with a look of delicious satisfaction. Teasing the dancers further, the *heyoka* holds the ladle right in front of the mouth of each in turn and lets the water trickle down onto the ground. This is the supreme temptation, which the dancers need to resist. The *heyoka*'s teasing is of course vexatious for the dancers, but in overcoming the temptation they attain renewed confidence and gain a second wind. Their vexatious view of the *heyoka* gives way, meanwhile, to a shared sense of comedy.

Benjamin Grant Purzycki, a cultural anthropologist, examines *heyoka* in considerable detail in the paper "Conceptions of Humor: Lakota (Sioux), Koestlerian, and Computational," which appeared in the journal *Nebraska Anthropologist* (volume 21, 2006).

Heyoka are the sacred clowns or contraries among the Sioux. These figures are, according to [Thomas H.] Lewis [in *The Medicine Men: Oglala Sioux Ceremony and Healing*], "loosely organized [and] at least partly [a] secret society . . . [and] by systematically breaking the customs and prohibitions of the community the contrary achieves a personal mysteriousness that translates into the magical and the sacred." It must be noted that this "breaking the customs" and violating taboos are sanctioned only insofar as the individual that actually breaks the custom is indeed a heyoka, even though some . . . still find them objectionable. In other words, these institutionalized rebels, through their actual breaking of the rules, are enforcers and perpetuators of the holy—in order for the clowns to fulfill their role or obligations as heyoka, they break the rules.

The Lakota *heyoka* John Fire Lame Deer (1903–1976) describes his vocation in the autobiographical *Lame Deer, Seeker of Visions*, which he wrote with Richard Erdoes (1912–2008). Lame Dear has this to say about *heyoka* in that work:

> [A *heyoka*] is an upside-down, backward-forward, yes-and-no-man, a contrary wise . . . Being a clown brings you honor, but also shame.

Purzycki provides further detail about the role of absurdity in the *heyoka*'s holy foolery in "Conceptions of Humor."

> When a contrary is asked a question, he will answer in opposites. [The *heyoka*] have been known to wear next to nothing in cold weather and wear far too much in hot weather, and they've been known to ride horses backwards in battles. Such is the life of a contrary. Traditionally, *heyoka* tended to dress in shabby clothes; some were reported to simply wear burlap sacks with eyeholes cut out in them. Masks the clowns sometimes wore/wear have exaggerated phallic noses, and their actions are typically full of sexual innuendo and flat-out mock performance of sexual acts. They were known to have lived in teepees with the tarps or skins on the inside with the frame exposed to the elements.

The absurdity is ultimately about laughter, about holy foolery. Lame Deer reminds us of the comforting power of laughter.

> For people who are as poor as us, who have lost everything, who had to endure so much death and sadness, laughter is a precious gift. When we were dying like flies from white man's disease, when we were driven into reservations, when the government rations did not arrive and we were starving, watching the pranks and capers of *heyoka* [was] a blessing. (*Lame Deer, Seeker of Visions*)

CHAPTER 7

Eminent Interpreters
of Foolery

Yanagita's disregard for utility

Studying the social role of laughter yields intriguing insights into
the development of our civilization. We are indebted once more
to Yanagita Kunio (1875–1962) for laying crucial groundwork.
His cultural conservatorship included cataloging numerous ways
that laughter has figured in the life of Japan over the centuries.
For example, Yanagita recorded instances of laughter fulfilling a
formal role in civil administration and in common law.

We saw in chapter 4 how villagers ostracized for prescribed
offenses could earn pardons by wandering through their villages and inviting the laughter of their neighbors (pages 68–69).
Yanagita cites an interesting role for laughter in contracts in
"Warai no bungaku no kigen" (The origins of the literature of
laughter). He refers to a provision sometimes included in 17th-
century lending agreements. Failure to repay the loan on time
would entail the humiliating punishment of absorbing peals of
laughter from the villagers.

Yanagita acknowledges in the preface to "Warai no hongan"(The vow of laughter) the pioneering work by the French philosopher Henri-Louis Bergson (1859–1941) in analyzing laughter. But he suggests that Asia's cultural heritage encompasses laughter unknown in the West. Yanagita cites several examples of Asian laughter worthy of study. Among his examples are the Chinese parable of the three laughs of Tiger Ravine; the rollicking fun of the legendary Tang dynasty (618–907) poets Hanshan and Shide; and the laughter of Yamaraja, the god of death in Hindu and Buddhist mythology.

The tale of the three laughs of Tiger Ravine is an allegory of the positive interaction of Buddhism, Daoism, and Confucianism. It describes an encounter by three historical figures, though their birth and death dates indicate that the story is apocryphal. The Buddhist monk Huiyuan (334–416) lived as a recluse beside Tiger Ravine, and he had vowed never to cross a stone bridge that led across the stream. He received occasional visits, however, from two good friends, the Daoist priest Lu Xiujing (406–477) and the Confucian poet Tao Yuanming (365–427).

Toward the end of one visit from Lu and Tao, Huiyuan walked his friends down the path away from his dwelling. So engrossed in conversation were the three that they had walked all the way across the bridge without noticing. Only after they had reached the far side of the ravine did they realize what had happened. The realization—some versions of the tale attribute their sudden awakening to a tiger's roar from the forest—triggered spontaneous laughter from all three. That laughter is an enduring, practical reminder of the importance of religious tolerance and understanding.

Hanshan (Cold Mountain) and Shide (Foundling) lived, according to legend, on the fringes of Guoqing Temple, in what is now Zhejiang Province. They received zen training and occasional sustenance from the temple master, Fenggan. Hundreds of poems attributed to the three—mainly to Hanshan—survive, and the authorship of the poems is a subject of continuing study and debate. The verses fairly resound with laughter, whether the poets are poking fun at the materialism of city dwellers or reveling in moments of zen awakening. Hanshan and Shide have long been a favored subject for Chinese and Japanese artists, and the

*Hanshan (Cold Mountain) and Shide
(Foundling)*
Chinese 14th-century ink drawing

paintings and drawings typically portray them grinning or laughing heartily. The infectious fun of the two holy fools helps us see through the illusory tyranny of our self-imposed burdens.

Yamaraja originated in Hindu mythology but is familiar to Chinese and Japanese primarily through his carryover into Buddhist mythology. Although he is a wrathful deity, artists over the centuries have frequently delighted in rendering him with a comical countenance. Laughter figures in some of the tales of the deity, and Saimyoji Temple, in Japan's Tochigi Prefecture, has a famous statue of a laughing Yamaraja. The comical tone conveys the Buddhist insight that even death is but a self-imposed delusion.

Yanagita despaired of finding the time to analyze and catalog his sources properly. And he expressed the fervent hope that future scholars would see fit to explore further along the trails that he had blazed. Yanagita was writing in December 1945, just four months after Japan's surrender in World War II. We can but marvel that he was pressing ahead with such research at all under such circumstances.

Let us marvel, too, at Yanagita's attention to endangered cultural assets. He worked tirelessly to gather and preserve even tidbits of dying traditions, abiding by a patient, cumulative approach. The traditions and practices under study coalesced on their own terms, and their tale of history and human development emerges organically through their gradual agglomeration.

Yanagita was sensitive to the potential long-term value of cultural assets of undetermined utility. Some of the endangered cultural assets that he collected were already obsolescent in the eyes of his contemporaries. Yet Yanagita pressed ahead with his conservatorship on behalf of posterity. He called for cherishing our cultural heritage and warned against discarding any part of that heritage casually. Witness his following comment on dialects in *Oko-no-bungaku* (The literature of foolery):

> Those who would meld dialects into a single "standard" tongue exhibit contempt for the dialects condemned to oblivion. That is foolish and is unacceptable in folkloric studies. If anything, cultural assets in danger of extinction should command all the more care and attention.

Today's scientific and academic establishments are lamentably unreceptive to the kind of work that Yanagita did. Recall the foregoing examples of laughter in village administration and in contracts. They suggest that laughter warrants at least a footnote in any history of Japanese jurisprudence. But I have been unable to find any Japanese law school that mentions the foregoing examples in its curriculum. Japan's law school curricula focus obsessively on equipping students to pass the bar examination. The educational establishment in contemporary Japan, like its research counterpart, has no use for cultural insights of less than compelling utilitarian value. So it allows historical vignettes like the application of laughter in legal sanctions to disappear from our collective memory.

In science, work in "leading-edge" sectors that promises immediate and tangible benefits receives overwhelming priority in employment and in funding. I see that firsthand in my "day job" at the Japan Society for the Promotion of Science. There, my work consists of routing research proposals through networks of professors and scientists for evaluation. Today's scientific establishment has little patience for a Yanagita-like approach of letting research findings mature and reveal their truths over time. It has still less patience for the study of things on the verge of obsolescence and thus, in the eyes of the establishment, irrelevance.

The increasingly shortsighted focus on immediate utility in awarding research funding threatens to undermine long-term scientific progress. Consider the breakthrough that earned a share of the 2008 Nobel Prize in Chemistry for Shimomura Osamu (1928–). Shimomura earned the Nobel recognition for his isolation of the photoprotein aequorin from the jellyfish *Aequorea victoria*. Aequorin generates blue light and together with green fluorescent protein produces *Aequorea victoria*'s distinctive green bioluminescence.

Shimomura's work has yielded immense practical value. The blue light emitted by aequorin is readily detectable with a luminometer, so the photoprotein has become a useful tool in molecular biology for measuring intracellular levels of ionic calcium. Green fluorescent protein, meanwhile, has proved invaluable in fluorescence microcopy and in gene therapy. Yet no one, least of all Shimomura himself, could have imagined any utilitarian benefits when the Japanese scientist began his research on bioluminescence in the 1950s.

Motivating Shimomura was an intellectual curiosity imbued with the spirit of pure science. His approach was one that, sadly, receives dwindling support from the scientific establishment, at least in Japan. Short-changing pure research diminishes the potential for the kinds of practical benefits that ultimately accrued from Shimomura's work.

In my concern about the outlook for scientific research, I have taken solace in following the Ig Nobel Prizes. Those prizes are a sort of holy foolery of science. And I take pride as a Japanese in the frequent Ig recognition for work by my compatriots. Here is a summary from the official website.

> The Ig Nobel Prizes honor achievements that make people LAUGH, and then THINK. The prizes are intended to celebrate the unusual, honor the imaginative—and spur people's interest in science, medicine, and technology.
> Every September, in a gala ceremony in Harvard's Sanders Theatre, 1,100 splendidly eccentric spectators watch the winners step forward to accept their Prizes. These are physically handed out by genuinely bemused genuine Nobel Laureates.

The Ig Nobel Prizes are the brainchild of the magazine *Annals of Improbable Research*, which bestows the awards. Cosponsoring the awards ceremony annually are the Harvard-Radcliffe Society of Physics Students and the Harvard-Radcliffe Science Fiction Association.

Some examples of prize-winning work by Japanese researchers are illustrative of the tone of the Ig Nobels. Two Japanese researchers won the acoustics prize in 2012 for developing the SpeechJammer, a device "that disrupts a person's speech, by making them hear their own spoken words at a very slight delay." And a team of seven Japanese researchers won the chemistry prize in 2011 "for determining the ideal density of airborne wasabi (pungent horseradish) to awaken sleeping people in case of a fire or other emergency, and for applying this knowledge to invent the *wasabi* alarm."

Among the earlier Ig Nobel laureates from Japan: the inventors of the Tamagotchi virtual creature, "for diverting millions of person-hours of work into the husbandry of virtual pets" (economics prize); the inventors of "Bow-Lingual, a computer-based automatic dog-to-human language translation device...for promoting peace and harmony between the species" (peace prize); the inventor of karaoke, for "providing an entirely new way for people to learn to tolerate each other" (peace prize); researchers who succeeded "in training pigeons to discriminate between the paintings of Picasso and those of Monet" (psychology prize); a researcher who developed "a way to extract vanillin—vanilla fragrance and flavoring—from cow dung" (chemistry prize); researchers who discovered "that slime molds can solve puzzles" (cognitive science prize).

[Translator's note: Japan's strong showing in the Ig Nobels has continued since the publication of the original, Japanese version of this book. A team of seven Japanese and Chinese researchers won the medicine prize in 2013 "for assessing the effect of listening to opera, on heart transplant patients who are mice." Also in 2013, a team of seven Japanese researchers won the chemistry prize "for discovering that the biochemical process by which onions make people cry is even more complicated than scientists previously realized." And four Japanese researchers won the physics prize in 2014 "for measuring the amount of friction between a shoe and a banana skin, and between a banana skin and the floor, when a person steps on a banana skin that's on the floor."]

I am heartened to know that Japan remains a font of research "that make[s] people LAUGH, and then THINK." For I believe that the long-term viability of Japanese science and technology depends on looking ever beyond immediate utility. And in the frolicking of holy foolery does that stance find its most vigorous expression.

Bergson's philosophy of laughter

The pioneering work by Bergson acknowledged by Yanagita appears in *Le Rire. Essai sur la signification du comique* (*Laughter. An Essay on the Meaning of the Comic*), published in 1900. That work, the title notwithstanding, is actually a collection of three essays. Yanagita's personal library of some 20,000 books includes the English translation, published in 1913. So we can surmise that Yanagita was among the work's earliest readers in Japan.

Yanagita was in good company in absorbing Bergson's thought. The French philosopher was hugely influential. He would receive the 1927 Nobel Prize in Literature "in recognition of his rich and

Henri-Louis Bergson (1859–1941) ✵

vitalizing ideas and the brilliant skill with which they have been presented." And he would receive in 1930 France's highest honor, the Grand-Croix de la Légion d'honneur. Bergson, who died of bronchitis in Nazi-occupied Paris at 81, also warrants our admiration for his faithfulness to his beliefs. A Jew in Vichy France, he was loath to accept exemption from the government's antisemitic laws and therefore renounced all the official posts and honors that he had received. Bergson even deferred a planned conversion to Catholicism to avoid giving the appearance of trying to escape the pogrom.

In *Laughter*, Bergson mulls, among other things, the stage comedies of Molière (1622–1673) and examines the causes of laughter from a physio-mechanical perspective. He discovers comic roots in imitation and attributes our resultant laughter to an implicit incongruity between life as lived naturally and arbitrary intrusions.

> I mean our gestures can only be imitated in their mechanical uniformity, and therefore exactly in what is alien to our living personality. To imitate anyone is to bring out the element of automatism he has allowed to creep into his person. And as this is the very essence of the ludicrous, it is no wonder that imitation gives rise to laughter. . . . This seems to me the solution of the little riddle propounded by [Blaise] Pascal [1623–1662] in one passage of his *Pensées* (*Thoughts*): "Two faces that are alike, although neither of them excites laughter by itself, make us laugh when together, on account of their likeness." . . . The truth is that a really living life should never repeat itself. Wherever there is repetition or complete similarity, we always suspect some mechanism at work behind the living.

Bergson thereby confirms the origin of his subject: "This deflection of life toward the mechanical is here the real cause of laughter."

Laughter is something of a curiosity in the larger context of Bergson's oeuvre. Just why the philosopher took up the subject briefly is a mystery. I suspect, however, that it had a lot to do with his daughter, Jeanne, who was born deaf in 1896. Bergson cherished Jeanne and helped his daughter fulfill her potential through artistic activity in painting and sculpture. We can well imagine Jeanne's presence would have weighed on him at the theater as he enjoyed the plays of Molière. And her deaf presence could well have inspired Bergson to probe beyond the audible in seeking the causes of laughter.

Yanagita's vow of laughter

The motivation for Yanagita in taking up the subject of laughter is clear and straightforward. Laughter had lost the central position, feared Yanagita, that it had traditionally occupied in the life of Japan. Animating "Warai no hongan" (The vow of laughter) is a powerful sense of concern about the implications for Japanese society of laughter's diminished role.

Japan's headlong pursuit of modernization and Westernization had long since sacrificed the nation's community-based agrarian culture to the cause of economic rationalization. People had come to regard holy foolery, which had enjoyed a respected position in traditional society, as mere foolishness. Driving the final nail in laughter's coffin was the nationwide mind control that accompanied wartime mobilization. Few cared anymore that holy fools might be more than mere jesters, that they might be seers in touch with a world and a future invisible to ordinary people. Japanese had their hands full with the all too visible world of the present.

Yanagita rued the future of a Japan bereft of holy foolery. The *hongan* of his essay's's title can mean "goal" or "desire," but Yanagita is using the term in the Buddhist sense of a bodhisattva's vow to save all living things. And Yanagita regarded holy foolery as essential to fulfilling the vow of salvation through laughter. He regarded his iconoclastic contemporaries Origuchi Shinobu (1887–1953; pages 8–9) and Minakata Kumagusu (1867–1941; pages 161–165) as contemporary incarnations of holy foolery and encouraged their activities in that spirit.

Fulfilling a vow of laughter was thus a core inspiration in Yanagita's trailblazing work in folkloric studies. Stoking that inspiration were inputs from diverse sources. Let us examine some of those inputs.

Hokusai Manga

Yanagita encountered the *Hokusai Manga* (page 116) as an adolescent. He discusses the encounter in *Kokyo nanajunen* (Seventy years of hometowns), a verbal memoir recorded by two reporters and published in 1959.

> [The series] consists of 15 volumes and is truly impressive. The 12th volume is especially memorable, a genuinely comical collection. It's full of incredibly funny sketches that you can't view without laughing. For example, one depicts [a] hooded fortune-teller intently examining the face of a beautiful woman through a magnifying glass. We see the woman's face magnified way out of proportion. The series is one wildly exaggerated rendering after another. . . . It all comes back to me hysterically as I describe the sketches.

We can readily see what so amused Yanagita on viewing the work described in the preceding passage, *Tengankyo* (Magnifying glass). The hairdo and apparel visible above and below the magnifying glass in ordinary perspective do indeed suggest an attractive woman. But the oversized nose and eyes seen through the magnifying glass are a comical deflection, as Bergson says, of the presumed beauty.

The other works in volume 12 are equally amusing; for example, a vendor of eyeglasses selling three lenses to a three-eyed ghost, a long-necked demon about to startle a blind lutist, an animate bolt of lightning that has injured itself on striking the earth, a long-nosed *tengu* demon manipulating its nose, a foot courier caught in a huge spider's web, a skinny sumo wrestler competing with himself. Volume 12 includes several works that poke fun at nobles and samurai. It underlines Hokusai's reputation as a pioneering artist in lampooning the ruling class.

The fortune-teller and magnifying glass that captured Yanagita Kunio's attention in volume 12 of Hokusai Manga

Katsushika Hokusai introduced to the world a new vein of laughter. He stretched the norms of perspective and explored the possibilities engendered by the pigments newly imported from Europe. Hokusai blended cultural elements of East and West in turning Japanese popular culture inside out and thereby exposed an astonishing, sometimes shocking, frequently hilarious, and ever-exhilarating *japonesque*.

Working in an Edo-period Japan (1603–1868) ostensibly isolated from the world, Hokusai was a quintessentially cosmopolitan artist. His work would exert immense influence on subsequent generations of Western artists. And that influence reflects Hokusai's absorption of developments in Western art. That Vincent Van Gogh (1853–1890) possessed some 400

Some of the curious beings portrayed in Hokusai Manga, *Volume 12*

ukiyo-e works is well known. What is less known but equally significant is that Hokusai was in the possession of a trove of Western etchings.

A preoccupation with perspective born of Western influences was a decisive influence in the birth and development of ukiyo-e prints. That influence arrived via technological contrivances, as well as through artworks. Although the shogunate had largely closed Japan off to foreign trade, limited commercial interchange continued with the West through the Dutch trading post of Dejima in Nagasaki, and Western goods also reached Japan through the continued interchange with China, Korea, and a few other trading partners. The arrival of microscopes and telescopes lent an unprecedented elasticity to perceptions of size and distance, and zograscope optical devices amplified the effect of perspective in flat pictures.

Meanwhile, imports of pigments and of chemical raw materials for pigments augmented artists' palettes. Prussian blue, for example, provided an affordable alternative to costly lapis lazuli–based blue pigments and allowed artists to render blues more freely in their work. Hokusai used the newly available Prussian blue to spectacular effect in his iconic *Beneath the Great Wave off Kanagawa* (early 1830s).

Heinrich Heine

A folklorist at heart, Yanagita eagerly absorbed the rich German tradition of folktales. He admired the work of the Grimm brothers, Jacob (1785–1863) and Wilhelm (1786–1859), in compiling their namesake collection of fairy tales. And he especially admired the work of the German poet, journalist, essayist, and literary critic Heinrich Heine (1797–1856).

We have seen (page 10) that the young Yanagita took note of Heine's essay "Die Götter im Exil" ("The Gods in Exile"). He also read and was profoundly impressed by a Heine essay on folklore entitled "Elementargeister" ("Elemental Spirits"). Yanagita found in Heine an invigorating revolutionary spirit whose stance resonated with the stance of the holy fools.

Heine accompanied romantic poetry with revolutionary politics, which made for something of an untenable combination. His politics frequently came between him and his literary counterparts, and his romantic attachment to European civilization prevented him from buying in fully to the notion of proletarian revolution. Heine's revolutionary bent was perhaps more aesthetic than political, a reflection of a fondness for going against the accepted wisdom and for upturning established values. That fondness is a fundamental trait of the holy fools, and it is apparent in Heine's frequently amusing observations. Yanagita loved the humor betrayed in the following kinds of aphorisms.

> Those who have drained the cup of joy in this world will have a hangover in the next.
> "Letzte Gedichte und Gedanken" ("Thoughts and Aphorisms")

> I cherished a deep horror of every occurrence, such as, perhaps, the night-wandering spirits of the dead experience; for these, it is said, are terrified when they meet a living man, as much as a living man is terrified when he meets a specter.
> "Florentinische Nächte" ("Florentine Nights")

> Unprecedented and fabulous were indeed the events of those crazy February days, when the wisdom of the wisest was brought to naught, and the chosen ones of imbecility were

raised aloft in triumph. The last became the first, and the lowliest became the highest. Matter, like thought, was turned upside down, and the world was topsy-turvy.

"Geständnisse" ("Confessions")

Born to a Jewish textile merchant in Düsseldorf, Heine was the eldest of four children. He demonstrated little acumen for business and entered the University of Bonn in 1919 to study law, shifting after a year to the University of Göttingen and later to the University of Berlin. Göttingen University was, interestingly, where the brothers Grimm would find employment in 1830, Jacob as a professor and head librarian and Wilhelm as a professor. There, they became, in 1837, two of the Göttingen Seven: a group of seven professors who protested the rewriting of the constitution of the Kingdom of Hanover and refused to pledge allegiance to the king and who lost their university positions as a result.

Heine became acquainted with the Grimms in Kassel in 1927 and reportedly admired their work. The Grimms had gained acclaim with their fairy tales despite criticism that some of the tales were inappropriate for children. Another, later criticism of *Grimms' Fairy Tales* was their anti-Semitic tone. We might wonder if Heine didn't find that tone off-putting. But his upbringing in Judaism had been casual and, in any event, he converted to Christianity in 1825. Discrimination against Jews was on the upswing in Prussia in the 1820s, and Heine would have been unable as a Jew to achieve his then aim of securing employment at a university. The conversion also reflected Heine's readiness to upset the established order, including the established order of his life.

France's July Revolution of 1830 lured Heine the following year to the liberating environment of Paris. Heine empathized with the revolutionaries and, too, was eager to escape the censorship that limited his writing in Germany. He was a popular figure in Paris and consorted with numerous luminaries there. Heine would spend the remaining quarter century of his life in Paris, though he never assimilated fully and felt to the end an outsider, a German among French.

Karl Marx (1818–1883), fleeing Prussian persecution, took up residence in Paris with his wife in 1843. He knew of and respected Heine and carried several of the latter's poems in a journal that he published in Paris. The two shared a contempt of the bourgeoisie, though Heine's romantic notions of revolution were at variance with Marx's scientific socialism. They developed a close relationship in Paris and corresponded after Marx's deportation to Belgium in 1845.

Part and parcel of the romanticism that set Heine apart from his fellow German expatriate Marx was a nostalgia for German's ancient spirituality. Heine had seen fit to convert from Judaism to Christianity in the context of social and professional necessity and in the context of personal transformation. He was at heart closer, however, to the ancient German spiritualism that Christianity had supplanted. And he was uncomfortable with the way that Christian intolerance had felled the native gods of his motherland. That spiritual orientation informed the revolutionary stance that captivated the young Yanagita and shaped his foundational work in folkloristics.

Yanagita regarded Japan's spirits and goblins as analogues of the fallen gods described by Heine in "Die Götter im Exil." They retained, in his eyes, vestiges of their former glory, as he writes in the essay "Hitotsume kozo" (One-eyed goblin): "Whenever an older faith is displaced by a newer one, its deities assume the standing of lesser spirits—an unofficial pantheon—in the new regime." Yanagita insisted, meanwhile, that this phenomena occurs in nations worldwide, "irrespective of ethnic context."

James Frazer

Revolution is the drama of social transition writ large, and revolution in traditional societies entailed the practice of regicide. We have seen that Yanagita took a strong interest in the role of holy foolery in testing the established order. That interest was part of his larger concern with the dynamics of social transition. A book that enthralled him with its accounts of regicide and regal succession was *The Golden Bough*, by the Scottish anthropologist Sir James George Frazer (pages 61–63).

Frazer was a native of Glasgow and graduated from the University of Glasgow in 1874. Reading Sir Edward Burnett Tylor's (1832–1917) *Primitive Culture* sparked in him an interest in social anthropology, and he pursued study and research in that field at Trinity College, Cambridge.

Getting rid of sovereigns who have outlived their usefulness is but a single facet of Frazer's stunningly multifaceted *Golden Bough*. The book is a comparative study of mythology and religion that examines those subjects in connection with a vast spectrum of cultures and eras. Frazer identifies intercultural commonalties in sacred and secular thought, and he examines numerous social practices in the course of his remarkable narrative.

The Golden Bough first appeared in 1890 as a 2-volume work. Its second edition, issued in 1900, comprised 3 volumes, and the third edition appeared in 12 volumes over the years 1906 to 1915. Frazer added a supplementary 13th volume in 1937. The title is a reference to a painting by the great British artist J. M. W. Turner (1775–1851) of a scene in Virgil's (70–19 BCE) *Aeneid*. In the painting, we see Aeneas and the Sibyl gaining admission to Hades by presenting the golden bough to the gatekeeper.

Frazer opens his preface to *The Golden Bough* with this modest statement of purpose: "The primary aim of this book is to explain the remarkable rule which regulated the succession to the priesthood of Diana at Aricia." We gain a stronger feel for his sense of purpose in the opening lines of chapter 1.

> Who does not know Turner's picture of the Golden Bough? The
> scene, suffused with the golden glow of imagination in which the

The Golden Bough, *exhibited 1834*
Painting by J. M. W. Turner (1775–1851)

divine mind of Turner steeped and transfigured even the fairest natural landscape, is a dream-like vision of the little woodland lake of Nemi—"Diana's Mirror," as it was called by the ancients. No one who has seen that calm water, lapped in a green hollow of the Alban hills, can ever forget it. The two characteristic Italian villages which slumber on its banks, and the equally Italian palace whose terraced gardens descend steeply to the lake, hardly break the stillness and even the solitariness of the scene. Diana herself might still linger by this lonely shore, still haunt these woodlands wild.

Yanagita began reading *The Golden Bough* in 1912 at the recommendation of Minakata Kumagusu. He describes his response to the book in the following excerpt from an interview:

Never have I experienced in reading any other book such rapture as I experienced in reading Frazer's *The Golden Bough*. I gained further inspiration from Frazer's [*Folklore in the Old Testament: Studies in Comparative Religion, Legend, and Law*], though I read just two-thirds of it and have not gotten around to finishing the book.

Looking back on [Frazer's] work, I am in awe of his careful attention to detail and at the impressive way he eschews any shortcuts in presenting his conclusions. I realize my immense debt to the man for alerting me to the importance of every detail, however small. The uncommon insights of Minakata Kumagusu come to mind, though they are perhaps less systematic. We can but be amazed at the unity that comes to the fore in a genuinely international perspective, at the commonality observed among different ethnic backgrounds.

Nagahashi Takusuke (1899–1975) handled the translation of the Japanese edition of *The Golden Bough* published in 1951 by Iwanami Shoten. He met the author to secure permission to publish the Japanese translation. And we learn from his commentary published with volume 5 of the Japanese translation of *The Golden Bough* that Yanagita had also met Frazer.

I don't know how much influence Yanagita, known as the father
of Japanese folkloristics, absorbed from [*The Golden Bough*].
(He expressed no special interest when I consulted with him
about publishing a Japanese translation.) I know, however, that
Yanagita read all 13 volumes, and I heard directly from Frazer
that Yanagita had paid him a visit.

Yanagita's "no special interest" seems at odds with the "rapture" cited in the foregoing quotation. Let us recall, however, that the discussion with the prospective translator Nagahashi presumably occurred during the war years. And let us peruse the following *Golden Bough* excerpt from chapter 17, "The Burden of Royalty," in that light (paragraphing added):

At a certain stage of early society the king or priest is often
thought to be endowed with supernatural powers or to be an
incarnation of a deity, and consistently with this belief the course
of nature is supposed to be more or less under his control, and
he is held responsible for bad weather, failure of the crops, and
similar calamities.

To some extent it appears to be assumed that the king's
power over nature, like that over his subjects and slaves, is
exerted through definite acts of will; and therefore if drought,
famine, pestilence, or storms arise, the people attribute the
misfortune to the negligence or guilt of their king, and punish him
accordingly with stripes and bonds, or, if he remains obdurate,
with deposition and death.

Sometimes, however, the course of nature, while regarded as
dependent on the king, is supposed to be partly independent
of his will. His person is considered, if we may express it so, as
the dynamical center of the universe, from which lines of force
radiate to all quarters of the heaven; so that any motion of his—
the turning of his head, the lifting of his hand—instantaneously
affects and may seriously disturb some part of nature.

He is the point of support on which hangs the balance of the
world, and the slightest irregularity on his part may overthrow the
delicate equipoise. The greatest care must, therefore, be taken
both by and of him; and his whole life, down to its minutest
details, must be so regulated that no act of his, voluntary or

involuntary, may disarrange or upset the established order of
nature.

Frazer refers to Japan's emperor throughout *The Golden
Bough*, using the term *mikado*, as an example of a ruler. The
notion of punishing the emperor "with stripes and bonds, or, if
he remains obdurate, with deposition and death" would not have
sat well with the wartime authorities. If Yanagita came across to
the prospective translator as unenthusiastic, his own concern with
"stripes and bonds" or worse might have been in play.

Minakata Kumagusu

Expertise in slime molds was among the attainments that distinguished Minakata Kumagusu. Those attainments transcend the
scope of this book, but let us note in passing that Minakata was
born in what is now Wakayama Prefecture in 1867, that he died
there in 1941, that he published 51 papers in the authoritative
scientific journal *Nature*, that he worked in a circus in Cuba while
collecting fungi samples there, that he lost his library privileges
at the British Museum for slugging a visitor for a racist slur, that
he lectured the emperor on slime molds, that he was a friend of
Sun Yat-sen (1866–1925), that he was a pioneering researcher in
human sexual behavior and led an openly homosexual life until
marrying a woman at the age of 41. May the reader take the initiative to investigate separately the reasons for Minakata's well-
deserved reputation as a protean thinker and an epochal eccentric.

Yanagita found himself in 1906 supporting the irrepressible
Minakata in a campaign against an ill-conceived government
edict. That was before Yanagita had abandoned the bureaucracy

and devoted himself to folkloric studies. He was then a counselor of the Cabinet Legislation Bureau.

The Japanese government had moved in the Meiji period (1868–1912) to strengthen central government control over the provinces. Shinto shrines were important focuses of community solidarity in towns and villages throughout the nation. So the government had called for consolidating the shrines in each of the nations' smaller municipalities into a single shrine. That would streamline the channels of control over the populace. It would dilute, however, the role of shrines as faces of natural phenomena. And Minakata feared especially that it would result in environmental pillage at the sites of former shrines.

Minakata rallied opposition to the edict, speaking out at public gatherings and dispatching letters to government figures and opinion leaders that detailed the problems with the edict. So aggressive was his oratory that he ended up in jail for 18 days after crashing a public gathering.

Yanagita became acquainted with Minakata after the latter's return from London in 1900. He queried Minakata about the mountain people of Wakayama and about other sociological matters, and Minakata responded in detail. Yanagita, still an official in the Cabinet Legislation Bureau, was a recipient of one of Minakata's letters in opposition to the shrine consolidation. And he cooperated by forwarding it to more-senior officials.

Minakata, in turn, became a frequent contributor to the folkloric journal that Yanagita launched in 1913. And Yanagita traveled to what is now Wakayama Prefecture at the end of that year to visit Minakata at his home. He recalled the visit in the previously cited *Kokyo nanajunen*.

When Yanagita arrived at Minakata's house, he received a message through the latter's wife that her husband would come to the inn where Yanagita was staying. Yanagita, puzzled, returned to the inn and waited, seemingly in vain. He went ahead with dinner, and Minakata had still not arrived when he finished. Yanagita asked the innkeeper if no word had arrived from Minakata, and the surprising response was, "He's already here." Minakata was shy about meeting people in person for the first time, and he had

Minakata Kumagusu (1867–1941)

prepared by imbibing in a back room at the inn. Yanagita later reported being impressed that Minakata "never repeated himself, no matter how much he drank." He added incredulously, however, that Minakata "didn't utter a word that night about anything of scientific importance."

Yanagita went again the next day to Minakata's house to pay his respects. The latter was drunk again and received his visitor in a curious manner, his face concealed in a robe. "I can't see a thing when I'm drunk," sounded a voice through a sleeve. "So I don't need to stick my face out as long as we can talk."

"He was as eccentric as they come," concluded Yanagita in his remembrance. Yanagita surely delighted in Minakata as a modern incarnation of the holy fools of old. He valued the latter's insights into comparative ethnology, meanwhile, and was forever grateful for the introduction to Frazer's *The Golden Bough*. The two ultimately parted ways, however, as Minakata's unrestrained handling of such subjects as sexuality, including homosexuality, exceeded Yanagita's tolerance.

Human behavior in any society was, for Minakata, an expression of a primordial life force and warranted study in that context. Yanagita, on the other hand, preferred to deal with human behavior in reference to the self-conscious pursuit of social progress. Witness this excerpt from "Warai no bungaku no kigen" (The origins of the literature of laughter).

> Among those who have studied laughter among primitive peoples is [the Hungarian-American psychoanalyst and anthropologist] Géza Róheim [1891–1953]. He reports that the Australian aborigines laugh aloud not only on triumphing in contests of strength but also on satisfying hunger or sexual desire and even on relieving the bowels. Róheim reports, too,

that the aborigines believe that their spirits also laugh heartily in similar circumstances. [People] smile at the thought of that vulgar laughter. That members of polite society find a source of amusement in such a subject is evidence not so much of social progress as of atavistic reversion. [How much we have truly progressed as a civilization and] our prospects for lasting peace and fulfillment are an issue that warrants careful attention from those who would make their livelihoods through the profession of writing.

Yanagita apparently regarded unconscious laughter triggered by physiological phenomena as a trait of the uncivilized. He seems to have regarded conscious, intellectual laughter as a bellwether of civilization. For Yanagita, even holy fools were responsible for fashioning and directing their laughter with a calculated sense of purpose.

CHAPTER 8

Natural Disasters and Transcendent Laughter

Holy foolery amid catastrophe

The cultural anthropologist Yamaguchi Masao (1931–2013), citing the influence of the Italian semiotician and novelist Umberto Eco (1932–), characterized culture as "the technology of confronting crisis." In that sense, we can position Japan's tradition of holy foolery as part of the social machinery for coping with catastrophe.

Japan has experienced more than its share of natural disasters over the centuries, including earthquakes, tsunami, volcanic eruptions, typhoons, floods, epidemics, and droughts. Each of those disasters has exposed critical failings in the Japanese establishment's capacity for responding to crises. And holy foolery has served repeatedly to partly offset those failings.

A standard in the repertoire of *rakugo* comedic storytelling is a work entitled *Tensai* (Natural disaster). The short-tempered Hachigoro shares a room with his wife in a shoddy string of apartments. One day, Hachigoro is beating his wife so in an altercation that his mother rushes from next door to intervene. Hachigoro, however, strikes even his mother in his uncontrollable fury and then takes refuge in the home of an elderly man in the neighborhood. The man is appalled at Hachigoro's conduct and refers him a respected counselor, providing a letter of introduction.

On reading the letter of introduction, the counselor voices a series of adages. They pertain to such subjects as the evils of short-temperedness, the virtue of patience, and the importance of parental piety. Hachigoro hasn't a clue, however, as to the meaning of the proverbs and responds with a blank look. That prompts the counselor to make his meaning clearer with a question-laden parable.

"What would you do," he asks, "if you were walking down the street and a house servant accidentally splashed water on your garments?"

"I'd beat him to a pulp," replies Hachigoro, "and complain to his master."

"What would you do if you were walking down the street and a roof tile fell and hit you?"

"I'd go in and let everyone have a piece of my mind."

"What if the place was vacant?

"I'd go find the landlord and let him have a piece of my mind."

The counselor can see that Hachigoro's idea of a solution to any problem is a full frontal assault. So he opts for a change of tack.

"What would you do if you were walking across a meadow and a sudden cloudburst drenched you to the skin. You've got no umbrella and no place to take shelter. What would you do?"

"Uh, I guess I'd just have to deal with being wet."

"But you'd've punched a house servant for splashing water on you."

"You can't pick a fight with the heavens for the rain."

"So why don't you just accept the water splashed by the servant or the tile that falls from the roof as a natural disaster? Wouldn't that make you happier with life?"

Hachigoro finally perceives the wisdom of the counselor's message. Thanking the counselor for the guidance, he goes home. No sooner has he returned, however, than an uproar erupts in a nearby room. A neighbor, Kumagoro, has tossed out his wife and brought home a new mate. Now, the former wife has returned and is lighting into her ex and his current housemate explosively. Emboldened with the wisdom imparted by the counselor, Hachigoro strides confidently onto the scene to broker a peace. He starts with the adages but makes such a hash of them that the warring threesome can but wince at his senseless utterances. Then, Hachigoro launches into the parable, with equally disastrous results.

"What would you do if you were walking across a meadow and a house servant accidentally splashed water on you . . . uh, no, if a house servant fell off of the roof and onto you . . . uh, wait a second . . ."

Hachigoro pulls himself together miraculously, however, for the conclusion. "All of these events are acts of god. And you can't pick a fight with the heavens." That admonishment sets the stage for the unfortunately untranslatable play on words of the punch line. Kumagoro replies that acts of god (*tensai*) are all well and good but that his pressing issue is the more prosaic matter of a former wife (*sensai*).

Fires and fisticuffs were the stuff of Edo culture. People were inclined to accept acts of god, however, as phenomena beyond the pale of human control. And that resignation figures in numerous comical works.

The philosopher Watsuji Tetsuro (1889–1960) detects a powerful influence from monsoon (typhoon) weather patterns in Japanese culture. He describes that influence in *Fudo* (*Climate and Culture: A Philosophical Study*). Watsuji attributes what he characterizes as "passive and subservient" tendencies among the Japanese to the seasonal yet sudden violence of the annual typhoons. Watsuji is surely right about the seasonal impact of typhoons and flooding on Japanese perspectives and values. But we should bear in mind, too, the impact of nonseasonal phenomena, such as earthquakes, tsunami, and volcanic eruptions.

Natural disasters, seasonal and otherwise, have clearly exercised a decisive influence on the Japanese psyche. The profundity of that influence finally registered with me only when I lived in Germany from 2004 to 2007. I resided in Bonn, but the event that changed my perspective on natural disasters was the flooding of Dresden by the River Elbe in 2004. That inundation, I was astounded to learn from the news, was the first such serious flooding there in 500 years.

I thought anew of the 1,000-year-old stone churches and castles and of the 800-year-old wooden houses and taverns that delight visitors to Germany. Few such structures could withstand Japan's earthquakes, tsunamis, and typhoons for a millennium. Germans have dealt, of course, with such natural disasters as North Sea flooding. But they know little of the acts of god that have afflicted Japan frequently and catastrophically throughout history. Japanese, by contrast, have come to accept as a fact of life a uniquely severe routine of natural disasters.

The word *disaster* is from the Middle French *desastre*, which is from the Latin prefix *dis-*, for "apart or asunder," and the Latin *astrum*, for "star." Disaster expresses the notion of deviation from the beneficence of the lucky stars. A natural disaster is, for the Europeans, an extraordinary event, a deviation from the norm. Conversely, calamitous acts of god are, for the Japanese, routine events.

Rituals—including festive laughter—were, for the ancient Japanese, means of elevating disaster from the profane to the sacred and thereby positioning calamity as an object of divine intervention. This is the proactive flipside of the "passive and subservient" aspect of the Japanese character cited by Watsuji. It is also Eco's "technology of confronting crisis."

Natural disasters in Japan's historical record

The eighth-century *Kojiki* (*Records of Ancient Matters*) details the birth of three pivotal deities. Izanagi had visited his deceased wife, Izanami, in the underworld and was performing a rite of cleansing on his return. On washing his left eye he spawned Amaterasu, the sun goddess. On washing his right eye he spawned Tsukuyomi, the moon god. And on washing his nose, he spawned Susa-no-o, the god of the sea and storms.

Susa-no-o differed from his siblings in his origin, born of nostril rather than eye, and in his wild demeanor. The etymology of his name is uncertain, but it wreaks of violence. Susa-no-o appears to have been a deification of violent weather.

Amaterasu became the ruler of Takama-ga-hara, the abode of the gods; Tsukuyomi of the nocturnal realm; and Susa-no-o of the sea. As we saw in chapter 2, Susa-no-o infuriated his sister by wreaking havoc in her realm. He destroyed the berms between Amaterasu's rice fields, filled in the irrigation ditches, defiled a sacred hall with feces, and tossed a pony onto Amaterasu's loom, killing one of her attendants. Amaterasu was so disgusted at her brother's behavior that she concealed herself in a cave. That cast the world into darkness and occasioned the hilariously lewd dance by Ame-no-uzume that lured Amaterasu back out into the open (pages 32–33).

The *Kojiki* and the *Nihon shoki* (*Chronicles of Japan*) include several descriptions of natural disasters. We find in the *Nihon shoki*, for example, the earliest documentation of an earthquake in Japan. "The earth shook," reports a passage, "on an autumn day in 416, during the reign of Emperor Ingyo." A legendary emperor, Ingyo reigned, according to tradition, from 410 to 453.

No mention of damage accompanies the reference to the 416 earthquake in the *Nihon shoki*. But the book is more informative about an earthquake that occurred in 599, during the reign of Empress Suiko (554–628, reigned 593–628).

> The earth shook, and buildings collapsed. An order went out [from the empress] to people everywhere to offer prayers to the god of earthquakes.

The *Nihon shoki* contains references to numerous earthquakes during the reign of Emperor Temmu (631–686, reigned 673–686). One is a description of an especially powerful quake that struck in December of the seventh year of Temmu's reign.

> The earth shook violently in Tsukushi Province [present-day
> Fukuoka Prefecture]. A fissure 2 *jo* [6.7 meters] wide and more
> than 3,000 *jo* [10 kilometers] long opened. Farmhouses collapsed
> in all the villages. One house was on a hill. It moved when the
> earthquake struck in the evening and the hill disintegrated.
> However, the house remained intact and undamaged. The people
> in the house did not notice that the hill had collapsed and their
> house had moved. But when they awakened [in the morning],
> they realized what had happened and were highly surprised.

Of the earthquakes reported in the *Nihon shoki*, the largest was
the Great Hakuho Earthquake of 684. The name is in reference to
the unofficial name of the era of Temmu's reign. That earthquake
produced Japan's first documented tsunami, as evidenced in the
following excerpt from the *Nihon shoki*:

> The earth shook violently at 10 p.m. Men and women of the
> region screamed in panic. The mountains crumbled, and the
> rivers overflowed. In all the provinces, too many to count were
> the losses of local-government buildings, farmers' granaries,
> temples, pagodas, and shrines. Countless, too, were the deaths
> of people and livestock. . . . In the province of Tosa, the sea
> swallowed some 500,000 fields. The old ones insisted that never
> before had the earth shaken so.

Let us note the compelling connection that people perceived
between earthquakes and divine will. That people regarded earthquakes as godly acts is evident in the sovereigns' responses to the
disasters. Empress Suiko, as noted, ordered "people everywhere
to offer prayers to the god of earthquakes. Emperor Temmu,
meanwhile, commanded prayers and offerings to the wind deity
at Tatsuta-taisha (Tatsuta Grand Shrine), in what is now Nara
Prefecture.

Kamo no Chomei and Henry David Thoreau

A literary classic of the Kamakura period (1185–1333) is an extended essay of 1212, *Hojoki* (*An Account of My Hut*), by Kamo no Chomei (1153 or 1155–1216). The author opens the essay with a lyrical observation on the transience of all things.

> Ceaselessly does the river flow, the water ever changing. Bubbles arise outside the current, bursting on the surface, others forming behind them, none lingering. Thus, too, in this world are people and dwellings.

Following this opening is a lengthy detailing of the tragedies that have befallen the then capital, Kyoto, including typhoons, tornadoes, famine, conflagration, and earthquakes. Here is an excerpt from Chomei's litany of disasters:

> A severe earthquake occurred. It was of extraordinary force. Mountains crumbled, rivers were blocked and the seas rose and inundated the land. The earth split open and water spewed forth. Boulders tumbled down into valleys.
>
> Boats along the shore drifted helplessly atop the waves, and horses on paths lost their footing. Not a single temple building or pagoda around the capital escaped damage completely. Some crumbled. Others toppled. Dust and ash rose like billowing smoke. The sound of the earth moving and of houses collapsing was like thunder.
>
> To be inside a house was to risk being crushed immediately. To run out was to encounter the crevasses that had opened in the earth. Lacking wings, people could hardly take flight. If only they could have taken to the clouds like dragons. The catastrophe reminded everyone emphatically that of all fearsome things, the most fearsome of all are earthquakes.

The narrative then describes how Chomei failed to attain the status he had envisioned for himself in Kyoto society and how he therefore opted to enter the priesthood, abandon court life, and become a recluse.

Chomei spent five restless years at the foot of Hiei-zan, a mountain that overlooks Kyoto from the northeast, and then moved to a site in the hills southeast of the city. There he built the hut of the title of his famous essay and lived out his days in quiet solitude.

Hojoki and its author invite comparisons to the 19th-century American classic *Walden* and its author, Henry David Thoreau (1817–1862). Like Chomei, Thoreau moved to the woods and lived in a cabin of his own making, though he lived there only two years. Thoreau's abode was near the Massachusetts pond of the book's title. *Walden*, originally published in 1854 as *Walden; or, Life in the Woods*, is in the form of a diary. Like Chomei in *Hojoki*, Thoreau accompanies the accounts of his daily activities

Henry David Thoreau (1817–1862) 🕸

with expansive philosophical explorations and probing personal reflections.

Minakata Kumagusu (1867–1941; pages 161–165) translated *Hojoki* into English at the urging of the British polymath Frederick Victor Dickins (1838–1915). The latter edited the translation extensively and provided its title: *A Japanese Thoreau of the Twelfth Century*. Dickins had worked as a surgeon and as a lawyer and had lived several years in Japan, where he mastered the language. He was working at the University of London as an administrator and Japanese scholar when he met and befriended Minakata. *A Japanese Thoreau of the Twelfth Century* appeared as a joint work by Minakata and Dickins in the April 1905 issue of *The Journal of the Royal Asiatic Society of Great Britain and Ireland*.

The high esteem that Minakata had earned in London is evident in a note that Dickins appended to their joint work.

> My friend Mr. Minakata is the most erudite Japanese I have met with—equally learned in the science and literature of the East and of the West. He has frequently contributed to *Nature* and *Notes and Queries* . . . The translation has been entirely remade by myself upon the basis of that of Mr. Minakata. The notes, save where otherwise indicated, are his, somewhat remodelled by myself.

Minakata's scholarly interests extended to the role of dwellings as modes of cultural expression, and he was surely sensitive to the parallels between *Walden* and *Hojoki* in that regard. Thoreau and Chomei each provide detailed descriptions of the construction of their dwellings.

Modes of homebuilding were an emphasis for the philosopher Watsuji Tetsuro. "The formalization of residential construction," he wrote in *Fudo* (*Climate and Culture: A Philosophical Study*), "is a form of human self-assertion in the context of climate and culture." Chomei and Thoreau each evince a strong sense of social context in describing the design and materials that they chose for their dwellings.

Having noted similarities between Chomei and Thoreau, let us note here a difference. Thoreau, as a member of the transcendentalist philosophical movement and as a student of the religious traditions of India, was alert to the ultimate transience of things material. But he exhibited a Yankee pride in his craftsmanship and in the durability of his cabin. Chomei, on the other hand, betrays no such preoccupation with the persistence of his architecture.

The difference between Thoreau's and Chomei's dwellings evidences a fundamental distinction in residential architecture. Yanagita Kunio (1875–1962) discusses that distinction in *Meiji Taisho shi—se so* (A history of the Meiji [1868–1912] and Taisho [1912–1926] periods—social trends). In Yanagita's interpretation, two basic modes of homebuilding arose early in human history, and those modes intermixed in Japan: (1) large structures built to last and (2) humble structures intended for temporary occupancy.

Differentiating the two modes is lifestyle, rather than wealth or social standing. City dwellers, rich or poor, generally resided in structures designed to afford some degree of permanence. Migratory peoples, on the other hand, lived in shelters, such as tents, that they could carry on their migrations or in simple shelters that they could construct readily from materials at hand.

In Japan and in several other nations, we find examples of people who used a combination of semipermanent homes in villages or cities and temporary residences for special purposes. The temporary residences might be for work, such as farming, fishing, or hunting, or for any of various other purposes, such as giving birth, for example, or undertaking festival preparations.

Japanese seem to have been less concerned than Westerners with permanence, even in dwellings ostensibly of the built-to-last mode. Only in recent decades have Japanese adopted urban housing of the kind of durability long common in Western nations. To be sure, the huge farmhouses seen in some parts of Japan served generation after generation over hundreds of years. But even those required the periodic replacement of their thatched roofs.

Constituting an important subset of impermanent accommodation are the lodging and shelters used through the ages by travelers. The great poet Matsuo Basho (1644–1694) prefaced his iconic travelogue of haiku, *Oku no hosomichi* (*The Narrow Road to the Deep North*), with a paean to travel as home.

> Eternal travelers are the sun and the moon, the passing years itinerants, too. For those who spend lifetimes floating on boats or who wander into old age while leading horses, every day is a journey, and the journey itself home. Many were the people of old who perished on the way.

Oku no hosomichi comprises prose and poetry written as a travel diary about a five-month journey in 1689. Basho undertook that journey, mainly on foot, through northern Honshu and along the Japan Sea coast. Accompanying him for most of the journey was his disciple Kawai Sora (1649–1710). *Oku no hosomichi* epitomizes the spirit of travel in Japanese literature. Origuchi Shinobu (1887–1953; pages 8–9) discusses that spirit in *Seze no hitobito* (People of different worlds).

[Well-to-do] travelers of old would erect lodgings for the night at each stop. They would hold parties and compose poetry in praise of the lodgings. . . . That tradition transcended travel, and people in each village would find an opportunity at least annually to undertake the renewal of an abode—to rebuild a house, perhaps, or to rethatch a roof—and to celebrate the outcome. The structures and their environs would invariably inspire poetry, and the resultant poetry was a vessel for the communal joy at the completion of the work.

Basho traveled in more modest circumstances than the sojourners that Origuchi perhaps had in mind, and he would probably have laughed at the notion of nightly parties. We'll take a look in a moment at one of the less-opulent lodgings that Basho and Kawai occupied during their journey.

Sei Shonagon and Yoshida Kenko

Natural disasters have been a continuous presence in Japanese literature, but their treatment has differed notably among historic periods. Let us examine the difference between Kamo no Chomei's response to destructive acts of god and the responses of two essayists that precede and succeed him chronologically: Sei Shonagon (966–1017 or 1025), best known as the author of the essay collection *Makura no soshi* (*The Pillow Book*), and Yoshida Kenko (1283?–1352?), best known as the author of the essay collection *Tsurezuregusa* (*Essays in Idleness*).

Sei Shonagon served in the imperial court as an attendant to Fujiwara no Teishi (977–1001), an empress consort of Emperor Ichijo (980–1011, reigned 986 to 1011). She was a contemporary and rival of Murasaki Shikibu (c. 978–c. 1014 or 1025), the author of *Genji monogatari* (*The Tale of Genji*) and an attendant to Ichijo's empress consort Fujiwara no Shoshi (988–1074).

Makura no soshi is a collection of observations and court gossip, frequently acerbic and consistently entertaining. The book's best-known portions are its numerous lists, such as the following example:

> Ungainly sights:
> A large ship beached at low tide.
> Large trees uprooted by the wind.
> An undistinguished man scolding a servant.
> A wife who ran off in a fit of jealousy, certain that her husband would make a fuss and come looking for her, and when he showed no sign of concern, found herself unable to stay in hiding and has returned home shamelessly.

Note in this example how uprooted trees—presumably blown over in a powerful typhoon—and a beached ship (possibly tossed onto shore by the typhoon) serve merely to set up the comment on an unhappy wife's awkward behavior. Sei Shonagon was painfully familiar with the catastrophic damage that natural disasters could wreak. She was 10 years old, for example, when a powerful earthquake destroyed large parts of Kyoto. And a typhoon ferocious enough to have uprooted large trees surely would have caused a great deal of harm to people and buildings. But adopting a stance apropos to the peak of the Heian period (794–1185), Sei Shonagon is more interested in the aesthetics of the typhoon than in its material or human toll. She wrote elsewhere in *Makura no soshi*, "If wind, let it be a storm," and waxed poetic about the sublime scenery on the morning after a typhoon.

Yoshida Kenko (1283?–1352?) was the son of a priest at a powerful shrine in Kyoto. He assumed a position in the court guards in his late teens and advanced in court rank through his 20s. However, he suddenly entered the Buddhist priesthood around the age of 30, though the reason for and the precise date of that career shift are unclear. Kenko was something of a peripatetic monk, occupying posts at temples in Kyoto, Kamakura, and Osaka. The date and even the place of his death are unknown, obscured by contradictory records.

Something that we most emphatically do know about Kenko is that he was keenly aware of *Genji monogatari*, *Makura no soshi*, and *Hojoki*, all of which he refers to in his writings. Something else that we know is that he was keenly aware of the horrors of natural disasters.

Kenko personally experienced severe earthquakes, fires, and floods. He lived, meanwhile, into the early years of the Nambokucho (northern and southern courts) period (1336–1392), when rival factions backed different claimants to the throne. Those experiences presumably shaped the sense of impermanence that Kenko expressed in *Tsurezuregusa* as "all things are illusory." Kenko accompanied his Buddhist sense of impermanence with an aesthetic sense that he consciously attributed to his Heian-period predecessors.

> How remarkable is the morning after a typhoon. To continue [in this vein] is to repeat what was written long ago in *Genji monogatari* and *Makura no soshi*, but I cannot resist expressing the same sentiments anew. So I let my brush run on, as dull as my observations might be, fit for discarding, unworthy of anyone's attention. (*Tsurezuregusa*, section 19)

We sense the influence or at least an awareness of Kamo no
Chomei, too, in *Tsurezuregusa*. That influence or awareness is
readily apparent in the following discussion of housing:

> A well and tastefully built house, though we know it to be but a
> temporary abode, is a source of pleasure. . . . How distressing
> and painful to the eye, however, is the sight of exquisite furniture,
> Chinese or Japanese, crafted with painstaking care by numerous
> artisans, arranged carelessly and [the sight] of the flowers and
> trees of the front garden left untended. No residency, of course,
> is eternal. And we can see all too easily that the house can turn
> to smoke in an instant. [But let us bear in mind that] a house
> reflects the character of its owner. (*Tsurezuregusa*, section 10)

Kenko's sense of impermanence differs from the "passive and
subservient" tendencies that the philosopher Watsuji Tetsuro
attributes to typhoons' influence on Japanese culture. For Kenko,
impermanence is a dynamic, positive phenomenon, something to
be approached from a proactive perspective. Shallow interpretations of the Buddhist concepts of emptiness and impermanence
tend to dwell on such aspects as mortality. Kenko, however, positions those concepts in the context of enabling life, as in the following passage:

> What a [calamitous] state of affairs we would face if the dew [of
> fragile life] never faded at Adashino moor, if the smoke [from the
> cremations] at Toribeyama moor ever ceased, if people lived
> forever. Life is all the better for the very uncertainty of its length.
> We are alone among the animals in our longevity. The mayfly
> lasts only until the evening. The cicadas of summer know not
> spring or even autumn. What could be better than to focus a
> lifetime on a year's existence? (*Tsurezuregusa*, section 7)

Although inclined to view impermanence in a positive light, Kenko was entirely capable of melancholia. He occasionally allows himself a sentimental reflection on life's transience.

> Like the depths and shallows of the Asukagawa river is life. Time passes, things wane, joy and sadness alternate. What was once a splendid quarter becomes an uninhabited moor. Where the houses are unaltered the occupants change. If the peaches and plums are mute, with whom are we to discuss the past? Ephemeral even are the ruins of great works unseen. (*Tsurezuregusa*, section 25)

Enlivening *Tsurezuregusa* throughout is Kenko's sense of humor. The author's laughter is sometimes caustic, sometimes more innocent. Here is a passage that elicits smiles with some deceptively profound kidding:

> Koretsugu no Chunagon [1266–1343] was a gifted poet. He was also a lifelong student of the [Buddhist] sutras, studying in residence under the temple master En-i [dates unknown]. Encountering the monk one day after the burning of [En-i's temple] Miidera in the Bumpo era [1317–1319], he quipped, "We have known you as 'temple master,' but now that you have no temple, we'll have to call you simply 'master.'" Now, that's a good line. (*Tsurezuregusa*, section 86)

Koretsugu is tapping the fount of holy foolery to express respect to and perhaps even to console his teacher. He reveres En-i for his teachings and guidance, not for his status as the head of a powerful temple.

Basho's *Oku no hosomichi*

Every day a journey, the journey itself home. The poet Matsuo
Basho embodied the spirit of travel that he described memorably in the preface to *Oku no hosomichi* and evoked throughout
that work. Inseparable from the act of travel in Basho's day was
hardship, and *Oku no hosomichi* provides revealing glimpses of
difficulties on the road. The episodes sometimes have a touch of
the comical, as in the following episode.

Here as throughout *Oku no hosomichi*, Basho sets the scene for
a haiku poem with a bit of background in prose. The name of the
checkpoint cited includes the Japanese word for what the horse
did all night beside Basho's pillow. Punning on place-names like
this is common in Basho's verse.

> After gazing up the road that leads to Nambu, we spent the
> night in the village of Iwade. We passed [the next day] by
> Ogurozaki and the islet of Mizu. Arriving via the Narugo hot
> spring at the Shitomae checkpoint, we prepared to cross over
> into the province of Dewa. But the guard at the checkpoint was
> suspicious, since few travelers use the road there, and only after
> a long delay were we able to pass through. Darkness fell as we
> climbed a large mountain, so we sought lodging when we came
> upon the home of a border guard. We thereupon had a spell of
> wind and rain that kept us there for three days.
>
> *Putting up with fleas*
> *and lice and the horse pissing*
> *right by my pillow*

Holy foolery on a bed of straw in the stable! Basho had
acquired plenty of experience with hardship before setting out on
the journey immortalized in *Oku no hosomichi*. He was in Edo
when a magnitude-8 earthquake struck the region in 1677. And

Matsuo Basho (1644–1694)
Ink drawing by Basho disciple Sugiyama Sampu (1647–1732)

he lost his simple hut of a home to a massive fire that consumed large parts of Edo in 1682. Those experiences reinforced Basho's professed disregard for permanent housing.

Natural disasters continued to shape people's worldview in the Japanese capital throughout the Edo period (1603–1868). Adversity occasions creative responses in thriving civilizations, and Edo culture spawned diverse means of coping materially and spiritually with catastrophe. One interesting response manifested in surges of popularity for different deities and cult-like practices. One practice consisted of collecting ukiyo-e woodblock prints of catfish, *namazu-e* (catfish pictures).

According to folk belief, catfish caused earthquakes by moving violently in underground lairs. A rumor spread in Edo after a powerful earthquake in autumn 1855 that *namazu-e* possessed magical powers for preventing earthquakes. And Edoites purchased huge quantities of the prints in the weeks after the quake.

The epicenter of the 1855 quake was directly under the capital, and the magnitude was a horrendously destructive 7.1. A vernacular magazine of the day reported that 200,000 people died in the quake, in the fires that engulfed entire neighborhoods in its wake, and in the tsunami that followed. That figure is an exaggeration by severalfold, as more reliable historical accounts place the death toll at less than 10,000. But the disaster was profoundly unsettling for the residents of the capital. And it prompted a widespread spiritual reaction among the populace, as seen in the phenomenal demand that arose for *namazu-e*.

Japanese had long regarded catfish as comical figures in the vein of holy foolery. But they had also associated catfish with earthquakes. And *namazu-e* evoked a combination of catfish's comical and horrific aspects. The Dutch anthropologist Cornelis Ouwehand (1920–1996) did extensive research on *namazu-e* for

Aftermath of the Great East Japan Earthquake of 2011

his doctoral thesis, published as *Namazu-e and their Themes: an interpretative approach to some aspects of Japanese folk religion.* Ouwehand was a seminal figure in the development of Japanese studies in Switzerland, where he taught at the University of Zurich. The original, English version of his book is unfortunately out of print, but the work is available in Japanese translation from the publisher Iwanami Shoten.

Lending weight to spiritual interpretations of the 1855 quake was the timing of the disaster. The earthquake occurred in the 10th month of the lunar calendar. That is, as we have seen (page 48), "the month of no gods." Legend held that the deities from throughout Japan gathered at the grand shrine of Izumo-taisha in that month and thus left the land without divine protection. Takemikazuchi was the deity responsible for keeping the catfish in check with a stone ballast. And people attributed the temblor to catfish running amok while Takemikazuchi was away at Izumo-taisha. Takemikazuchi appears in a lot of the *namazu-e*, sometimes seen restraining a huge catfish with the ballast stone, sometimes rushing back from Izumo-taisha to restore order.

Let us note how associating earthquakes with "the month of no gods" imparted a sense of periodicity to the seismic disasters. It allowed for grasping them in the same dimension as typhoons, Japan's seasonal threat. It elevated them into the realm of seasonal ritual, of special, deified events. That might not have done anything to ameliorate earthquakes' destructive force. And it didn't actually have anything to do with objective, geophysical reality. But the notion might well have served in some way, however small, to help people come to terms with the horror of seismic catastrophe.

Spontaneous laughter

Laughter in daily life includes the unconscious outbursts of physiological response to stimuli and the intentional laughter of cultural and social interaction. Even the laughter of holy foolery can arise unconsciously or intentionally. Spontaneous laughter is born of the collective unconscious, what Carl Gustav Jung (1875–1961) called the transpersonal unconscious.

The physicist, essayist, and haiku poet Terada Torahiko (1878–1935) made some interesting observations on intentional and spontaneous laughter. Terada's essays span a vast range, encompassing such diverse topics as science, cinema, haiku, *manga* comics, and, in one short work, laughter. In the essay on laughter, the author recalls a disinclination to laugh at objects that elicited laughter from others and, conversely, inexplicable laughter when devoid of any apparent object.

> I wasn't the least bit inclined to laugh at the gestures and antics of the village idiot. Rather, I felt uncomfortable and sad. Nor have I ever much felt the urge to laugh along with the other guests at the parlor tricks exhibited at drinking gatherings. I have had the experience of laughter welling up inside me, however, at the sight of trees bending and leaves and branches flying about in a violent gale. My voice has seemed at those times a natural complement to the noise of the storm. Similarly, I have experienced spontaneous laughter when wading through knee-high floodwaters as the frigid cold of the water pulsated through my entire body.

Terada, incidentally, wrote several essays on the theme of disasters. Informing those works is the author's personal experience in the Great Kanto Earthquake of 1923. That quake and the ensuing fires and tsunami devastated Tokyo and took more than 100,000 lives in and around the city. Terada's insightful and instructive essays on natural disasters remain pertinent, and they have become the subject of renewed attention in the wake of the Great East Japan Earthquake of 2011. Writers have cited his essays extensively in new scholarly papers about disasters and disaster response, and editors have included several of his essays in new compilations on those themes.

The spontaneous laughter described by Terada is redolent of the threshold between "the other world" and this world. That is a boundary traditionally bridged by holy foolery. To come to terms with unconscious laughter, we need to come to terms with at least the notion of "the other world." But scientific rationalism has all but extinguished that notion from contemporary society. And a landscape littered with human-made goods, permeated by the Internet, and governed by deadlines is scarcely amenable terrain for rediscovering our lost spirituality.

Spiritual rediscovery requires reconciliation with the natural world. The American mythologist Joseph Campbell (1904–1987) described that reconciliation in terms of securing "a sacred place" removed from the exigencies of daily life.

> [Having a sacred place] is an absolute necessity for anybody today. You must have a room, or a certain hour or so a day, where you don't know what was in the newspapers that morning, you don't know who your friends are, you don't know what you owe anybody, you don't know what anybody owes to you. This is a place where you can simply experience and bring forth what you are and what you might be. This is the place of creative incubation. At first you may find that nothing happens there. But if you have a sacred place and use it, something eventually will happen. . . . People claim the land by creating sacred sites, by mythologizing the animals and plants—they invest the land with spiritual powers. It becomes like a temple, a place for meditation.

We have seen (page 46) that the cultural anthropologist Yamaguchi Masao (1931–2013) suggested in *Warai to itsudatsu* (Laughter and deviation) that laughter originated partly as a means of overcoming trepidation. Yamaguchi suggested elsewhere that schizophrenics resort to laughter as a defensive measure to avoid slipping over the edge. He regarded both laughter and psychosis as naked efflorescences of the unconscious.

Biological and anthropological explanations of laughter are useful as far as they go. But they don't go nearly far enough in elucidating spontaneous laughter's origins in the unconscious. The French anthropologist Claude Lévi-Strauss (1908–2009) reappraised myth, positioning it as thought exercised by the unconscious. We need to do likewise with laughter. We need to reappraise the phenomenon of spontaneous laughter, positioning it as communication exercised by the unconscious.

Laughter as a cultural reaction

We turn now from spontaneous laughter to the conscious laughter of social and cultural intercourse. The latter comprises collective instincts exercised through responses in accordance with historical and social background. Those responses unfold in conformance with rigorous behavioral conventions.

Holy foolery has frequently functioned, as we have seen, as a response to natural disasters. And we need to recognize that response as a cultural reaction, as laughter of the zeitgeist. We need to be alert, too, to the implicit dichotomy of the profane and the sacred in people's perceptions of their environment. Laughter inherits that dualism in fulfilling its role as a cultural reaction.

The Dutch historian Johan Huizinga (1872–1945) examines the social function of frolic in *Homo Ludens. Versuch einer Bestimmung des Spielelements der kultur* (*Homo Ludens, a Study of the Play Element in Culture*). He argues that individuals' social life in ancient times took shape in reference to the comparative and ultimately confrontational context of the community.

Huizinga discovers an integral connection between frolic and sacred rites. He discovers the roots of frolic in the interplay of (1) the gravity of the rites, their temporal and spatial criteria, and their rigorous rules and (2) the urge for freedom. And that same interplay shaped the development of laughter as a social and cultural reaction.

Yanagita Kunio expresses a similar interpretation in the essay "Warai no kyoiku" (Laughter education).

> Song was a vehicle for cooperation as people joined voices in prayerful words for the deities and in spells for evil spirits. Ridicule was a vehicle for domination as people sought to position their rivals as laughable and their allies to do the laughing. I assume that [using ridicule] frequently avoided the need for resorting to arms [in securing the upper hand].

Origuchi Shinobu expresses the same interpretation from a different standpoint in the essay "Geino no hassei" (The birth of art).

Henri-Louis Bergson (1859–1941) and his successors in laughter studies have focused on historical cross-sections of social structure in interpreting laughter as a cultural reaction. That approach is insufficient, however, to account for the cultural reaction role of laughter in the life of Japan.

The philosopher Umehara Takeshi (1925–) takes exception in *Warai no kozo* (The structure of laughter) to Bergson's assertions in *Le Rire. Essai sur la signification du comique* (*Laughter. An Essay on the Meaning of the Comic*). Umehara complains that Bergson's various characterizations of laughter fail to encompass the full scope of the causes of unconscious laughter.

Yet Umehara's own analysis of laughter is, in the end, simply a variation on Bergson's. The latter's interpretation of laughter as a social reaction fails to account fully for the role of laughter in Japanese cosmology and in Japanese notions of interchange with "the other world." Umehara is an important figure in Japanese thought, and we can but wish that he had devoted more attention to applying and critiquing Bergson's theory of laughter in a Japanese context.

The unknown and the unknowable

Japanese before the modern era accepted the existence of "the other world"—the realm of the spirit—as a fact of life. Laughter possessed the power to dissolve the fear that arose in people's relationship with that realm. It possessed the power to transform the profane into the sacred, and achieving that transformation was precisely the role of the holy fools through the ages, as posited by Yanagita Kunio.

My preoccupation with laughter stems from revulsion at the rigid uniformity that the modern era has imposed on values. I look to laughter as a means of shattering that uniformity and of restoring a diversity of values to the world. In laughter born of Jung's "transpersonal unconscious" resides the potential for rediscovering the spirit of bilateral and multilateral interdependence.

Something of the unknown is intrinsic to laughter born of the unconscious. This fundamental aspect of laughter was of special concern to the French philosopher Georges Bataille (1897–1962). He discusses that subject in the lecture "Nonknowledge, Laughter, and Tears," which appears in a collection of English translations published as *The Unfinished System of Nonknowledge*.

> The unknown is obviously always unforeseeable. One of the most remarkable aspects of the domain of the unforeseeable unknown is given in the laughable, in the objects that excite in us this effect of intimate overturning, of suffocating surprise, that we call laughter. . . . The laughable always remains unknown, a kind of unknown that invades us suddenly, that overturns our habitual course, and that produces in us this "abrupt broadening of the face," these "explosive noises from the larynx," and these "rhythmic jolts of the thorax and abdomen" that doctors talk about.

Georges Bataille (1897–1962)

Having associated laughter with "the unforeseeable unknown," Bataille proceeds to assert further that what is laughable is unknowable, that the unknown is by its very opacity the cause of laughter.

> Suppose that the laughable is not only unknown, but unknowable. We still have to envision a possibility. The laughable could simply be *the unknowable*. In other words, the unknown character of the laughable would not be accidental, but essential. We would laugh, not for a reason that we would not happen to know, for lack of information, or for want of sufficient penetration, but because *the unknown makes us laugh*.

Parsing the workings of a mechanism immersed in the unknowable is a daunting task. But the stakes are high. "I told myself," recalls Bataille, "that if I happened to know what laughter was, I would know everything, I would have resolved the problem of philosophies."

Bataille brought a new and original perspective to his inquiry into the nature of laughter. Sadly, he died before illuminating his subject as much as he had apparently hoped to do. Let us hope that others will pick up where he left off. For laughter is our last, best hope for loosening the grip of bland uniformity on the industrialized world. And fulfilling that hope will hinge on rediscovering throughout society the magic of mirth.

Author's Afterword

I hope that my meanderings have helped illuminate the role played over the centuries by Japan's holy fools. Let me recount the holy fools' chief characteristics.

The aural dimension has been especially important. Holy fools have served foremost as hearers of the sounds that bridge "the other world" and "this world." They have interpreted the words of the deities and have absorbed sacred input not readily amenable to verbalization.

Another characteristic common to holy fools through the ages has been a peaceful, nonaggressive stance. Complementing that stance in numerous instances has been an extreme vulnerability. The holy fools have asserted sometimes surprising strength, however, through their capacity for the comical. And that capacity reflects a devotion to serving the common good, including a readiness for self-sacrifice.

Yet another characteristic of the holy fools has been their contrarian value systems. The holy fools have consistently thumbed their noses at the values of conventional society and have marched to the beat of a different drummer.

Japan's tradition of holy foolery is something that I have long regarded as a priceless cultural asset. Yanagita Kunio (1875–1962) described that asset convincingly and eloquently in his writings, and I was interested in calling attention anew to his insights into holy foolery. My day job and other commitments delayed the start of work on this book. But I finally went to work in earnest on the project, prompted in spring 2011 by the Great East Japan Earthquake and the ensuing tsunami and nuclear power plant disaster.

Natural disasters have figured prominently and repeatedly in Japanese history, as I describe in chapter 8. The events of 2011, however, accompanied the natural disasters of temblor and tidal wave with the human-caused disaster at the Fukushima Daiichi Nuclear Power Plant. Holy foolery had been invaluable in helping Japanese cope with past disasters. Rediscovering and recapturing the power of holy foolery, I reasoned, could help inspire and motivate people as they undertook the daunting reconstruction effort.

A voice that resonated along with Yanagita's in my head as I went to work on this book was that of the poet, author, and social activist of northern Japan Miyazawa Kenji (1896–1933). Lines of his famous poem "Unswayed by the Rain" kept coming back to me as I studied Japan's holy fools.

> Someone regarded as useless by all,
> praised by none,
> despised by none,
> that's the someone
> that I would be

I sensed a commonality between the "someone" that Miyazawa would be and Yanagita's notion of holy foolery. That sense of commonality rendered all the more poignant Yanagita's lamentation on laughter's diminished status.

> The most conspicuous signs of laughter's downfall have been the transformation of [the social standing of] the holy fools to [mere] idiots and the general tendency to regard [the formerly positive equivalent of "holy fool"] *baka* as a synonym for moron or dimwit.

Although Yanagita lamented the fate of laughter in Japanese society, he was optimistic that a field of ethnic studies focused on laughter would emerge one day. He envisioned that field of studies as a foundation for restoring holy foolery to its former standing.

Let us hope that future researchers in ethnic and folkloric studies will fulfill Yanagita's vision. For society needs holy foolery more than ever. The race-to-the-bottom competition of globalization has undermined the values that once defined societies in their interaction with each other. The headlong pursuit of economic gain has diverted production from its proper role in enhancing the quality of life. The obsession with utility for the sake of utility has robbed us of intangibles essential to a humanly well-rounded existence.

Holy foolery delights, as we have seen repeatedly, in lampooning the prevailing values of its host community. To the extent that a community's values are fundamentally sound, the lampooning is an opportunity for reaffirming those values. On the other hand, lampooning can expose values that have become corrupted. Our age is rife with the sort of perverted values that steered us onto the self-destructive course epitomized by the Fukushima Daiichi Nuclear Power Plant.

Henry David Thoreau (1817–1862; pages 175–177) spent a night in jail in 1846 for refusing to pay the poll tax. Thoreau's refusal was on account of his opposition to the Mexican-American

War and slavery. His incarceration was brief because someone, possibly his aunt, paid the tax on his behalf. But the incident spawned the tale of Thoreau's friend the essayist Ralph Waldo Emerson (1803–1882) visiting him in jail. The tale is apparently apocryphal, but that in no way lessens its message. Emerson asks his friend, "What are you doing in there, Henry?" To which Thoreau responds, "What are you doing out there, Waldo?"

When the legal world is acting insanely and immorally, the only sane and moral place to be is in jail. Holy foolery is serious business when the ostensibly serious world is acting foolishly. Holy fools are the voice of reason when the voice of the establishment is unreasonable.

Globalization is homogenizing all in its path, leaving holy foolery and other indigestibles buried under its slag heap of ejecta. A heart still beats in the corpus of holy foolery, however, and voices arise—persistent though faint—from the throats of the holy fools. Those of us who long for a world re-enchanted with holy foolery have but to perk up our ears. Hearing the voices anew, let us take heed and take part in reclaiming our world from the clutches of the truly insane.

"What do you have planned next?" The questioner was the prominent religious scholar Yamaori Tetsuo (1931–). We were at the 2010 awards ceremony for an essay contest sponsored by a Kyoto-based religious newspaper. I had won the top prize with an essay about the French philosopher Henri-Louis Bergson (1859–1941). Yamaori was one of the judges. "I've been meaning to write something," I blurted out, "about Yanagita Kunio's theory of laughter."

I had crossed the Rubicon. What I'd been meaning to do I'd finally expressed aloud. Now, I had to get to work. The project started slowly, as noted above, but gathered steam after the disastrous events of March 11, 2011. What resulted from my efforts, for better or for worse, is what you now have in your hands.

To everyone who helped bring this book about, I express heartfelt gratitude. And I dedicate the book to the victims and survivors of the Great East Japan Earthquake.

INDEX

A

Abe Juri, 136–137; *Amerika senju-min no seishin sekai* (The spiritual world of the American indigenous peoples), 136

Abe Kinya: "Chusei ni okeru shi" (Death in the Middle Ages), 71

absolution, 69, 70

abstinence, 85, 86–87

absurdity, 106, 134, 138

agriculture: *dotaku* used in rituals for, 14; laughter's value for, 41–42; as origin of laughter rite, 43–44; resident deities and land for, 29–30

Alcock, Rutherford: bemoans Japanese propensity to lie, 100; *Capital of the Tycoon, The: A Narrative of a Three Years' Residence in Japan*, 100

-ami suffix, 96

amanojaku (little ogres), 92

Amaterasu: ancestral goddess of Japan's imperial house, 6; cave myth of, 32–33, 34, 39, 40, 41, 43, 172; enshrined at Ise-jingu, 41; Himiko as, 22; lumpfish and, 60; as ruler of abode of gods, 172; spawned from Izanagi's eye, 171; Susa-no-o damages realm of, 132, 172

Ame-no-uzume, 32–33, 39, 40; depictions of, 33; laughter elicited by, 40; lewd dance of, 172; masks and, 33; saves world, 33

analogs, 60

ancestral spirits, 86

Anrakuan Sakuden: *Seisuisho* (Laughter for curing drowsiness), 106–107

antipathy, 128

April Fools, 101–102

Aristotle, 1, 94

artisans and merchants, 96, 97

ascetically diligent businesspersons, 127. *See also* Webber, Max, and Bataille, George: on imputing value to utility

Asian laughter, 140–142

Atsuta-jingu shrine, 44, 45, 46

audible, 7, 10, 149

aural dimension, 195

aural to visual shift, 21, 22

auspicious items, 117

auspicious sites, 119

authority, 22, 94

B

Bataille, Georges: imputing value to utility, 127; *La Part maudite, I: La Consommation* (*The Accursed Share: An Essay on General*

201

798

497

as ethnology of gods, 36; gender confusion in, 50–51; *Golden Bough* a comparative study of, 157; Hindu, 142; laughter as dynamic of, 36; midwinter rites in, 35–36; mirror central to, 21; realm of, 37; role of lightning in, 5; thunder god in, 6

N

Nagahashi Takusuke, 159–160
Nakazawa Shin-ichi: *Midori no shi-honron* (Green capitalism), 128
namazu-e (catfish pictures): blend of comic and horrific, 186; earthquake prevention powers of, 185, 186; Takemikazuchi in, 187
native gods, 156
Natsume Soseki, 105
natural disasters, 167–194; Bassho and, 184–185; continuous presence in Japanese literature, 179; decisive influence on Japanese psyche, 170–171; described in *Kojiki* and *Nihon shoki*, 172–173; extraordinary events for Europeans, 171; holy foolery a response to, 190; Japanese accept routine set of, 171; prominent in Japanese history, 196; shape worldview, 185; Sei Shonagon and Yoshida Kenko aware of, 180, 181; treatment varies historically, 179
New Year's: April Fool's Day and, 101; Ebisu and "noseless Ebisu" rite of first laugh, 40–41; families develop tradition of laughter at,

118; games become popular at, 115 (*see also Fukuwarai*); shrine visits and monetary offerings at, 30, 31; ubiquitous decoration for, 26 (*see also kadomatsu*)
nighttime rite, 44, 46
Nihon shoki (*Chronicles of Japan*), 15, 50 172; barbarians and, 18; Chinese accounts predate, 19 (*see also Sanguozhi*; Kuzu customs in, 16; male and female deities in, 92
Niu-jinja shrine: laughter festival at, 46; laughter festival's origins, 48; Niutsuhime patron saint of, 48
Niutsuhime, 46–47, 48
Noh: Kyogen comical counterpart to, 105; Greek tragedy and, 73; tragic and spiritual context of, 73
nonaggression, 195
noro, 23

O

O-bon festival, 23, 86; changed in reference to death, 87; dual role of, 87; as epitome of other-world belief, 26; refrain from work during, 86
Ochikubo monogatari (*The Tale of the Lady Ochikubo*), 77
offerings, 27, 30; of ceremonial laughter, 39; laughter long a part of, 65–66; parry menace and secure blessings, 28–30; weeping and laughing as, 73
Ojin (emperor). *See* Kuzu villagers: Emperor Ojin's encounter with
Okinawan shrines. *See utaki*

About the Author

A career devoted to coordinating scientific research has sensitized Higuchi Kazunori to the limitations of Western approaches to scientific inquiry. Higuchi went to work at the Japan Society for the Promotion of Science in 1984 after earning a degree in law from Tokyo Metropolitan University. His work there has centered on international exchange and on the allocation of research grants, and he has served postings at the society's offices in Washington, D.C., and Bonn. In parallel with his professional activity in connection with scientific research, Higuchi has studied and written about society's prescientific underpinnings in folklore. The author is a native of Tokyo, where he was born in 1959.

Apart from the Japanese original of *Holy Foolery in the Life of Japan*, Higuchi has published a book about Native American wisdom, *Gurandofaza no okurimono—toshi bummei wo koete—seinaru wa ni ikiru* (Gift of the grandfather—transcending urban civilization and living the sacred circle [Tokyo: Shimpusha, 2002]). An essay by Higuchi, "Ari no Berukuson, shuwa suru tetsugakusha—shinka ni seimei no choyaku wo mita otoko" (Bergson, ants, and observations on life's leaps), received the prestigious Ruikotsusho award in 2010. That award, presented by the religious newspaper *Chugainippoh*, recognizes distinguished writing on spiritual subjects.